AIN'T MIS-BEHAVIN'

The 10 Discipline Issues Every Parent Faces and How to Resolve Them

by William P. Garvey, Ph.D.

Adams Media Corporation
Holbrook, Massachusetts

To my grandchildren, Kimberly and Jeffrey, with the wish that
all children have parents like theirs.

Published by
Adams Media Corporation
260 Center Street, Holbrook, MA 02343

ISBN: 1-55850-805-8

Printed in the United States of America.

J I H G F E D C B A

Library of Congress Cataloging-in-Publication Data
Garvey, Ph.D., William P.
Ain't misbehavin' / William P. Garvey, Ph.D.
ISBN 1-55850-805-8
Includes index.
1. Discipline of children. 2. Child rearing. 3. Parent and child.
4. Parenting. I. Title.
HQ770.4.G37   1998
649'.64—dc21   97-44725
CIP

This publication is designed to provide accurate and authoritative information with
regard to the subject matter covered. It is sold with the understanding that the pub-
lisher is not engaged in rendering legal, accounting, or other professional advice. If
legal advice or other expert assistance is required, the services of a competent professional person should be sought.
— From a *Declaration of Principles* jointly adopted by a Committee of the
American Bar Association and a Committee of Publishers and Associations

This book is available at quantity discounts for bulk purchases.
For information, call 1-800-872-5627 (in Massachusetts, 781-767-8100).

Visit our home page at http://www.adamsmedia.com

Contents

Acknowledgments

If Dr. Gary Dolowich, healer extraordinaire, had not encouraged me at the beginning, this book would not have been written.

Hal Zina Bennett helped with the early stages of the manuscript and provided focus.

Laurence Greene, educator, author of numerous books, and most of all, my friend, provided practical suggestions and an unwavering enthusiasm that helped me to stay on track.

My wife, Joyce, read all versions of the manuscript. I cannot thank her enough for supporting me to undertake this project in the first place and for her heroic patience throughout.

The Challenge of Getting Kids to Cooperate

*I*n the late 1920's the legendary musician Fats Waller wrote a tune about being so much in love that the lover promised to stay at home and never misbehave. As a psychologist who has worked with hundreds of families, every now and then I think: wouldn't parenting be a breeze if our kids were like the person in that romantic song from yesteryear?—always good and loving, always loyal and respectful! We can hope, but just as the song is a fantasy, so too is the expectation that children be loving and cooperative all the time. Even the best-running families are in a constant state of "loving" tension. Parents set limits for the good of their children, and children test the limits. It is an age-old struggle, and one that happens at all ages. And it is a completely normal and natural part of growing up. In fact, it is so normal and natural that I've concluded that this testing and resisting of parents must be a child's job.

Having listened to many parents' stories and having raised three children myself, I know how tough it is when there are ongoing discipline problems. We anguish over problems, question ourselves, and at times even doubt our self-worth. You might be surprised to know how many parents have said to me, "Maybe I'm just not cut out for this." While I certainly know the feeling and sympathize with it, I usually reassure them by saying, "It has nothing to do with your abilities as a parent." So what is the reason? It is surprisingly easy to fall into patterns that produce misbehavior. Often they just creep up on parents in subtle ways, and before you know it, you have a problem on your hands. To make changes, you have to know how to identify these patterns.

Almost every parent who comes to see me has the *same* complaints: "He won't obey me." "She is impossible to control." "He has tantrums." "She won't do her homework." "She tells me no before I ask."

The problems that you have in handling your children, therefore, are really not unique to you, although this is not to say they are not challenging. Every parent faces these challenges, and the purpose of this book is to make the solutions to them easier for both you and your children. In this book you will find specific strategies to deal with a wide variety of discipline situations and a systematic program to handle children who have gotten out of parental control and are hard to manage.

The most important thing I have learned in nearly thirty years of helping parents resolve discipline issues and build happier families is that when kids consistently misbehave, they develop resistive and oppositional ways of talking and relating. They whine or argue or talk back or defy or yell or use any number of tricks, attempting to throw you off balance. These ways of resisting become their automatic response to discipline. What I have found is that, while setting limits on children's behavior is important, the key to successful discipline lies in managing the way kids talk and relate as they are being disciplined.

Usually we think of discipline as the process of setting rules and consequences to train children to obey. It does mean this, but there is more to it. In order for rules and consequences to work, you and your child need to relate effectively. When you do, the chances are greatly increased that the process of disciplining your children—having them listen to you and follow your directions and rules—will go well, and your relationship will be closer and more enjoyable.

Until fifty or so years ago, parents taught their children to talk respectfully to adults. They did not tolerate back talk and impudence, to use the terms of the time. For the most part, children were more cooperative and compliant than they are now.

Some people will argue that parents in those days were too restrictive, and perhaps they were. There is no question that parents should allow and encourage their children to express themselves. Stating one's thoughts, needs, desires, and disagreements is empowering. But we need to help our children create a workable balance between self-expression and respect for others. While this is not an easy thing to do, the goal is more than worthwhile, because when kids achieve this balance, they learn not only to relate well to others but also to be in control of themselves at the same time.

Relating is not one-sided. As parents we need to be respectful of our children as well, and we need to know how to relate constructively during discipline. This mutual respect helps build a child's self-esteem and goes a long way toward our feeling good about parenting.

LOOK AT THE BIG PICTURE

Parents usually want specific answers to specific questions. In the talks I give, I am asked questions like, "How do I get my child to go to bed?" "How do I get her to pick up after herself?" "How do I get him to come home on time?" If I always had clear, unqualified answers to these questions, I would be ecstatic.

Although specific answers can be helpful—and there will be specific answers in this book—they can also be misleading. Therefore, the first time I am asked one of these questions in a talk, I usually reply, "I'm not sure." As my audience starts to wonder why they have come to listen to this so-called expert, an awkward silence ensues.

However, I believe that if a problem is big enough for a parent to ask about it in public, chances are there is more to it. This doesn't mean that every problem is necessarily a big one or is widespread, and we don't want to create problems where there aren't any, but problems are often more complicated than they at first seem. So I need to employ my Sherlock Holmes approach, just in case.

Let's look at bedtime, one of the most "popular" areas that parents ask about. Problems with bedtime center around getting children to go to bed in the first place and then getting them to stay down. The little rascals shuffle off to bed and then shuffle back. Then, after some discussion, they shuffle off to bed again, and on and on it goes into the wee hours. This is the famous or, depending on your point of view, the infamous, "bedtime shuffle."

The first consideration with bedtime is to be sure there is not something physical that is causing a child to have difficulty in getting to sleep, or something emotional, like being scared, or an ongoing problem in the child's life that you may not know about, perhaps a problem at school. Once I've made sure parents have eliminated these issues, I ask what the rules and consequences are for bedtime. I go on to explain that the problem at bedtime is probably some kind of resistance. Then I pop the old sixty-four dollar question: "Does this resistance show up anywhere else?"

Is the problem bedtime, or is it resistance?

Sometimes parents are able to see difficulties in one area, but not in others, at least not until they are asked the right question. If you define the problem incorrectly, you will not be able to solve it. In this particular example, you need to find out if the problem is bigger than bedtime. If your child doesn't get over his resistance to bedtime in a reasonable amount of time, let's say a week or two, and there are no physical or emotional causes for it, check to see if there is resistance in other areas. For example, if your child doesn't do her homework, what else is she not doing? Chores? Coming home on time? If you find there are similar problems elsewhere, there is probably some kind of a pattern. Take it as a signal to look beyond the specific issue, to how you manage your child in general.

Susan and Frank described the bedtime problem they were having with seven-year-old Alex:

> "At first he wouldn't go down," said Susan. "He would make excuses, like he wasn't feeling well, and then he would stall. Can you imagine this? Once he even started to clean his room, right at bedtime, just before he knew we were going to tell him he had to go to bed. He said he wouldn't be able to sleep if his room was dirty."
>
> "I finally put my foot down," Frank added. "And he went to bed without any fuss for two or three days, but then he started getting up. He needed to go to the bathroom. He wanted a drink. He forgot to tell us something. Or there was a monster in his room."
>
> "How did you handle it?" I asked.
>
> "Well, at first, we thought he might be really scared," replied Susan, "and we comforted him. But after a couple of nights, it became clear it was one of his ploys. But we still don't get him down to stay until 9:30 or 10:00, and occasionally much later. This has been going on for nearly three months."

"I try not to get mad or yell," said Frank. "But it is pretty frustrating."

"Do you have any other problems with him?"

"Well, he's pretty demanding," answered Frank. "He doesn't ask nicely. He's kind of bossy."

"And he argues with me all the time," interjected Susan. "It's hard for me to get him to do his chores."

Susan and Frank looked at each other and shook their heads.

This is often the case. It isn't just bedtime that is the problem. Alex was becoming difficult to manage in a number of ways and was developing an oppositional style of relating. It wasn't too bad as yet, but it is the kind of situation that can escalate, if not checked. It is important not only to deal with the specific issue but also to see the context in which a particular problem occurs.

The silver lining in the dark cloud of discovering that a problem shows up in a variety of ways is that you will be able to get at its root faster and prevent its escalation, because you will actually have more opportunities to deal with it and, thus, change the behavior. And, if you have a systematic approach, it will be easier to deal with than you think. (Some strategies for bedtime are given in Part Three.)

NO GUILT, PLEASE

Many parents suffer from parental guilt, and they suffer needlessly. It's incredibly easy to feel guilty about your kids. First of all, you want the very best for them. You want them to be good in school, to develop their talents, and to have friends. You want them to grow up to be happy, mature, capable people. You don't want anything to go wrong. And you don't want anything to interfere with your dreams for your children.

Moreover, as parents, you can't escape the fact that you have an enormous influence over them. When they're little, you are their world. You shape their values, their attitudes, their biases, their beliefs, and even their personalities, to some extent. It's scary. There are many opportunities for you to feel guilty about your kids when things aren't going right.

Falling into the cesspool of guilt will not help. Guilt will eat you alive. It can destroy your good feelings about yourself, it can take away your confidence in your childrearing abilities, it can make you question everything you're doing as a parent, and it can make you feel like you're doing a bad job. It can even make you depressed. Here are some suggestions to counter guilt:

1. Be sure your standards for yourself as a parent are reasonable and appropriate. If they're too high, they will become impossible to meet, and you will feel like you are not doing things right. For example, while it's great to support your kids in what they are doing, you don't have to go to every single activity. It always amazes me that many parents feel terribly guilty if they miss a game during the soccer or baseball season. Of course, go to your kids' games; just don't be compulsive about it. Kids should do these activities for themselves, not for their parents or for the praise of their parents.

2. Don't nitpick every little thing you are doing as a parent. Being PERFECT is *not* required to do a good job. You *will* make mistakes. It is impossible not to. If you encounter information in this book that runs contrary to what you are doing, simply make whatever changes you feel are appropriate and go on. And remember, children are incredibly resilient. I often tell parents, "Look, I'm a psychologist, and I made my share of mistakes. My kids, who are grown now, turned out fine, and so will yours."

3. When you find you have made a mistake, don't indict yourself. Don't put yourself on trial. Don't go into a

long, inner harangue, telling yourself what a terrible parent you are, that you should never have had kids in the first place, and that you really don't deserve to live on this planet. Give yourself a break.

Many years ago, I heard a story about how to deal with that inner critic, who can make us feel bad about ourselves. Our inner relationship with ourselves needs to be like the relationship between the automatic pilot and the navigational system on a big jet. The automatic pilot flies the plane, and the navigational system keeps the plane on course. If the plane gets a little low or drifts a little to starboard, the navigational system sends a signal, a message to the auto pilot, which then makes the needed correction.

The message from the navigational system is clear and to the point: "You're down 200 feet and need to pull up." "You need to turn 2 degrees to port." It doesn't say, "You're down 200 feet, dummy!" Or, "You're off 2 degrees. Where did you learn to fly this plane? What's the matter with you? You should never have been a pilot."

Be objective with yourself and as nonjudgmental as possible. Of course, give yourself feedback on what you are doing as a parent. But feedback is just that. It's information about your parenting that you assess and then make changes accordingly. Self-blame and condemnation are not objective feedback. They only make it harder for you to make changes. Do whatever you can to stop blaming yourself and feeling guilty about mistakes. You'll feel a lot better about yourself as a parent and as a person.

RELATIONSHIPS IN THE FAMILY

Many parents wish they had a better relationship with their children. In spite of their good intentions and diligent efforts to make things go well, they feel deeply disappointed that they and their children do not get along, I have found that many of the relationship problems that parents and children have stem from the negative interactions during discipline. When we address the style of relating and make changes there *first*, however, the whole pattern of difficult behavior often changes very quickly. Moreover, once these interactions start going well, the overall relationship between parents and child improve, and everyone in the family is happier.

Finally, when parents know how to discipline effectively, the act of disciplining their children, although trying at times, can be a positive experience for all. As a parent, you can have the satisfaction of training your kids to be mature, responsible, and ultimately successful members of society. You can also have the satisfaction of creating a constructive, close relationship with them, one that wears well with the years. How you go about the act of disciplining your child in ordinary, day-to-day situations will have a lot to do with the attainment of those satisfactions.

As you will see in the last two chapters of this book, children who are well disciplined are responsible, and responsible kids are more resourceful and competent than those who are not. As a result, they like themselves and have good self-esteem.

I have also learned over the years that the same methods that work with your little kids also work with your young teenagers, up to about thirteen or fourteen years old. Therefore, although I have written this book mainly for parents of younger children, the same methods can be used for dealing with older children as well.

PART ONE

Identifying and Understanding Styles of Relating During Discipline

You can't discipline your kids and not relate to them. This is obvious; but what may not be so obvious is how much impact the way you and your children relate has on the outcome of discipline.

Since discipline takes place in an interaction between you and your child, *how* you interact strongly affects the outcome of any disciplinary intervention on your part. When you and your child relate and interact effectively, the chances of discipline working are greatly increased. When you relate poorly, for example, when you yell at each other, discipline usually doesn't work very well. Moreover, what is important is the pattern of this relating over time. Isolated incidents of poor relating are not as important as what takes place typically on a daily basis.

Chapter One examines how you as a parent relate to your children. What is your style of parenting? The chapter defines a style that works and describes eight different styles that are ineffective.

Chapter Two focuses on how your kids talk and relate to you. Do they interact appropriately with you when you set limits or correct them, or do they argue or whine or become belligerent? Do your children have an oppositional style of relating? And if so, how do you handle it? Moreover, how can you prevent such a style from developing in the first place?

CHAPTER ONE

What Is your Parenting Style?

*I*n order to discipline effectively, you must have a parenting style that works. What this really means is that you must relate well to your children as you are disciplining them. You simply can't be effective if you don't. Effective relating gets discipline moving in a positive direction. It helps reduce adversarial positions, it establishes a constructive and supportive emotional tone, and it makes resolving conflicts much easier. Relating is the cornerstone of discipline.

Moreover, we have to start with ourselves first. Before we can change misbehavior in our kids, we have to be certain that our own approach to them is effective and constructive.

Take a good, close look at yourself and your approach to disciplining your children. Look at your style and your emotional reactions when you are dealing with your children. Try to do this without judgment and without self-blame. Remember the story of the automatic pilot and navigational system in the Introduction. You want your guidance system to give you the feedback you need without negative comment.

Like so many things in life, discipline and child rearing can become routine. Without realizing it, we can easily fall into a rut, reacting without thinking about what we're doing. We all do this. So take your parenting style off of automatic for a while and reflect on it. Notice its impact. Evaluate its overall effectiveness, and make changes if necessary.

When a child is disobedient and difficult, sometimes the problem lies in the parents' management style. Yet many parents are not aware of their parenting style and its effect. For example, one style that does not work so well is the "pleaser." As we will see later in the chapter, this style can set up problems because it creates a tendency to give in to a child's demands and in the process to give up parental authority. When parents become aware of this style, and how they give their power away, it becomes possible to give up the pleaser pattern and become more assertive. Discipline then goes much better.

Therefore, as you read this chapter, rather than assume that you know your style, press the slow-motion button on the VCR of your life with your children. Step back and take a fresh look at the way you manage your kids. Put the action on pause, or replay it several times. Do whatever is necessary to get an objective look at your management style.

Although every parent's way of managing his or her children is different, there are several general questions you can ask yourself. Are you strict, or are you permissive? Do you make choices for your kids, or do you let them make choices? How much freedom do you give your kids? How accountable must they be? And, most importantly, how do you relate to them when you discipline them? As you read this chapter and watch yourself in your interaction with your children, keep these questions in mind.

Before we look at styles in more detail, two areas are important to consider: the issues of love and authority in disciplining children.

LOVE IS NOT ENOUGH

While it goes without saying that children must be disciplined with love, sometimes parents think that all they need to do is love them and everything will turn out all right. After we had discussed the management problems she was having with her eight-year-old son, David, Karen told me rather dejectedly: "I don't understand why I have so many problems with David. Why won't he obey me? My husband and I love him very much, and we tell him that constantly. Besides, he has just about everything he wants. I don't mean we spoil him, but he has many opportunities to do things—he goes to camp, and takes piano lessons and gymnastics. There isn't anything we wouldn't do to give him a good life."

It is not possible to overstate how important it is to provide for kids and give them love. But when it comes to discipline, love is not enough. You must have a consistent approach to handling issues as they come up and an effective management style. Karen was having problems with David, not because she didn't love him or David didn't know that she loved him, but because her style of managing him was not effective. When she realized this, she was able to change her parenting style, and David stopped misbehaving.

PARENTAL AUTHORITY: YOU MUST BE IN CHARGE

In my professional practice over the years, I have helped hundreds of parents who were having difficulty managing their children. In the vast majority of cases, the central problem was that the parents had unwittingly surrendered too much of their power to their kids.

Giving children too much power never works. Kids will just do what they want and not develop an inner sense of responsibility, which is necessary in order to become a mature adult.

Of course, I know these parents didn't just hand control over to their kids. They didn't say, "Here. You run things for a while. I'm too tired. I'm going to the beach." Subtly, in little ways that didn't seem to matter at the time, they gave in to their kids' demands. Giving in is like erosion on a hillside. You lose a little soil here and a little there, and one day the whole hillside goes. You give in here, you give in there, and all of a sudden your child is having temper tantrums (and in the supermarket, to boot). It's important to understand how this happens. It never happens out of the blue, even though it may seem like it. It is absolutely necessary for you to be in control of your children. You cannot run a smooth, happy household unless you are the final authority.

When you are in control of your children, you set limits for them. You determine the boundaries in which they can operate. As we'll see in more detail in Chapter Three, because they cannot do this very well for themselves, a very important kind of security is provided for kids in this way.

The younger the child, the more specifically you must define these boundaries. Children can then feel safe because their world is defined for them, something they cannot do for themselves. These kids clearly know where the limits are. As they grow older, the boundaries become smaller and fewer.

For a variety of reasons, some parents are reluctant to be in charge. They fear being harsh, repressive, or authoritarian. As a result, they become too lenient, and their kids gain too much power.

Other parents relinquish their authority because they don't want to see their children in any kind of discomfort. (A surprising number of parents feel this way.) For example, they are reluctant to punish and to have their children suffer the consequences, or they may believe it is too painful for their children not to get what they want. As a result, they become too lenient, and their kids gain too much power.

Still other parents are afraid to be the authority because they believe that their children won't learn to think for themselves and become truly independent. As a result, they are too lenient, and their kids gain too much power.

Being in control does not mean you have to be repressive or squash your child's independent thinking. Repressiveness and squashing come about not from being the authority, but from *how* authority is exercised. Authority is not inherently repressive. You can be the boss without being bossy. You can be in charge in calm, gentle, and loving ways.

Being in charge does mean that you will sometimes make your kids uncomfortable about not getting what they want. However, is this so bad? One of the things children need to learn as they grow up is that they can live with discomfort; they can live with not getting what they want, and the world does not come to a screeching halt.

When kids have too much power in the family, they often become fearful and insecure. This insecurity shows up mainly in two ways:

1. They become anxious (a kind of unspecified, but pervasive fear). You'll see this in restlessness and increased levels of activity.
2. They begin to act up. They test you more and more, by pushing against the limits, first at home and then, if unchecked, in other settings.

Kids are not going to tell you this, of course, and their behavior would seem to indicate otherwise, but they are unhappy when they have too much power in the family—and you are, too. Children need you to be in charge, because they don't know what they're doing. (They may think they do, but they don't!) They really do need boundaries and limits. One of the main jobs of parents is to provide these limits.

Often we don't provide sufficient limits because of our own upbringing. A few years ago, Alan, the father of Derrick, age seven, described to me how he had grown up. His father was a dictator. "He ordered us around constantly. If we crossed him in some way, even when we didn't mean to, he would get angry and yell. He never hit us or anything like that, but I was really scared of him. There was only one way to do things, and that was his way. We didn't dare get out of line. It was like boot camp."

Alan was never allowed to think for himself and grew up frightened of his father. Determined not to do the same thing to his children, he went too far in the other direction. He seldom commanded his kids to do things and hardly ever gave them consequences for misbehavior. Without realizing it, he was shunning his authority. As a result, his children, especially Derrick, became unruly and uncooperative.

When Alan realized that he was overcompensating for his own childhood, he became more comfortable in his role as the authority and was able to make changes in the way he managed his children. He understood that being the authority did not mean he had to be authoritarian. He learned to be firm and to give consequences in a loving, gentle way, and his children learned that he meant what he said.

Resolve Today to Be in Charge of Your Children

Before you can make any changes, you must have the intention and the commitment to accomplish your goal. Create this mind-set, right now: "It is in my own and my children's best interests that I am in charge of them." Ask for support from spouse and friends in accomplishing this goal.

Therefore, when it comes to managing your child, the question is not *whether* you will be in charge, but *how* you will be in charge. How do you exercise your authority, so that your children grow into the mature, responsible adults you want them to be? In this book you will learn to manage your children in a calm, loving, and fair way. You do not have to be punitive or use force to be in control of your children. You simply need the right methods.

WHAT THE EXPERTS TELL US

Psychologists and child-development specialists have conducted many studies about parenting styles. The main area they have focused on is the authoritarian-permissive dimension and how it affects children. What they have found is that extremes do not work very well.

An authoritarian approach is one in which parents try to shape and control children. Obedience is stressed, verbal give-and-take is discouraged, and the parent prefers a punitive, forceful type of discipline. Studies have found that children in these families tend to be more discontented, withdrawn, and distrustful of others than their peers.

At the other extreme, a permissive approach is both non-punitive and accepting, and kids are allowed to regulate their own behavior as much as possible. The parents, however, make few demands in the way of responsibilities and orderly behavior. The children in these families tend to be less self-reliant, explorative, and self-controlled.

The researchers found another type of parenting, which they call authoritative—as distinguished from authoritarian. In this approach parents provide firm direction for a child's activities, but give children considerable freedom within some reasonable overall limits. Parental control is present, but it is not rigid or unnecessarily punitive and restrictive. Parents provide reasons for what they require, and allow discussion and verbal give-and-take. This approach seems to have the best results. The children in these families are self-reliant, self-controlled, explorative, and contented.

GENTLE FIRMNESS: THE STYLE THAT WORKS

When you discipline your children, you are attempting to teach them something—to be on time, to talk respectfully, to do their chores, and so on. To get your teachings across to your kids effectively, you need a style of parenting that enhances their ability to learn from the discipline you are administering at any given time. The best way I have found to do this, and to implement the authoritative approach, is to use a style that I call "gentle firmness."

Firmness means making sure that the rules and consequences are clear to your kids and that you stand firmly by them. Your power lies in the rules and consequences. While you allow your kids to tell you their opinions, you generally do not allow them to talk you out of your decisions. You stand solid and unwavering. This does not mean you are unduly rigid or do not listen to your children, but you keep the limits and boundaries constant. Your children then know where they stand and what to expect from you. In this important way they can then rely on you.

Gentleness means that as much as possible you are warm in your approach. You are calm and relaxed. You do not yell or threaten or intimidate. You understand when your kids don't like a rule, for example, that they have to be home right after school, but you have good reasons for it. You stand by the rules and their consequences, and simply put them into effect when problems arise. But it is done gently and caringly. There is no need to be forceful. When the consequences kick in, life then teaches them their lessons. You let them know that you realize that it is hard for them when they can't have what they want.

This approach will avoid a lot of conflicts, because it treats kids with respect while you as the parent remain in charge. Let's look at an example: Mom has a rule that eight-year-old Mary must set the table each night.

"Mary, it's time to set the table for dinner."
"Mom, I can't. I have to call Jennifer."
"You can call her after dinner because we are going to eat in a few minutes."
"Mom, I *really* have to call Jennifer now."

This is a choice point for Mom. What can she do in this situation? Here are some options:

She can threaten: "Mary, you set the table this instant or you will not be able to spend Friday night at Jan's."
She can intimidate: "Mary (yelling), you set the table right this moment or you will be grounded for a week."
She can plead: "Mary, please set the table and help your mother. I don't have to do everything around here, do I?" (A little guilt is thrown in for good measure.)

None of these styles will work in the long run. They will all create problems.

Using the firm, gentle approach, here is what Mom did:

"Mary, what is the rule about setting the table?"
"If I don't set the table, I can't watch TV tonight."
"That's right. I know you want to call Jennifer, but you know the rule. What are you going to do?"

Mary set the table because Mom stuck to her guns. She stood firm with her rule and let Mary make the choice. She was calm and gentle. It worked, and it will work most of the time.

Having a positive, constructive style of discipline does not mean that you are always, in every single situation, perfect in your approach to discipline. Of course there will be times when you are angry, when you threaten, and when you give in when you shouldn't. A variety of circumstances can make it difficult to be smooth and consistent in managing kids.

But remember that we are talking about styles, the automatic and usual ways we interact. We want our styles to be positive and constructive, knowing that we cannot be perfect—and we do not have to be.

Most of us base our parenting styles on what we grew up with. While sometimes this is clear to us, often these styles that we have automatically adopted are not the best. *It is crucial to consciously employ a parenting and management style that works.*

The first step is to eliminate styles that do not work. Following are eight styles that create various kinds of problems with discipline. Check your style against these. If you find that you have one of them, then you can change your parenting approach in any way that you feel is necessary. Doing this exercise is not for the purpose of making anyone feel like a bad parent. After all, no one sat you down and told you that your parenting style would cause some problems for you. So just be open minded, and see if there is anything for you to learn here. The more awareness you have, the more resourceful you can be.

The Threatener

This style employs the liberal use of threats. "If you don't take out the garbage right now, you will be grounded for a week." "If you don't clean your room, you can't go to the movies this week (or for a month)." Parents who use this style of managing their children are usually frustrated and are reacting to that frustration without thinking.

On the one hand, these parents tend to make the threats too big; and on the other, they often don't really mean what they say. Thus, they don't follow through, and their threats turn out to be idle. You can't fool kids, at least not for long. They see through these things very quickly. The message the threatener is giving to kids is "I'm blowing off steam and don't mean what I say." Kids pay attention to our actions, not to our words. Then when the child becomes less cooperative, the parent tends to multiply the threats, but still fails to follow through, losing even more credibility with the kids. "I can't get them to do anything" is a common complaint of parents using this approach. The parents typically feel frustrated and helpless.

Rather than using threats, calmly tell your kids what the consequence is for a particular behavior. "Derrick, you know the consequence for not taking the garbage out is that you can't go outside to play until you do. It is up to you." You state the consequence calmly and let the consequence handle it. No idle threats, but a reasonable consequence that you will enforce. It works like a charm.

The Nag

The nagging parent is anticipating problems and is trying to avoid trouble. "Did you take out the garbage yet? C'mon, Derrick you know you're supposed to take out the garbage on Thursdays," and, five minutes later, "Derrick, have you taken out the garbage?" This scenario may run on and on for hours. Or, "Is your homework done yet? You know you have a test in spelling tomorrow." "You know you've got to study your spelling." This is repeated many times. Or, for the third time on a given morning, "Be sure to come home on time today after school. You've got to come home on time."

Parents who nag are worried about negative consequences happening to their child. They may be concerned their child will perform poorly on a test or that the child might miss out on something by being late. So they worry and they nag. They may also worry that they will have to punish their child for not obeying, as in the garbage situation, and they don't want to punish or be the bad guy. So they get on their kids, hoping that they can avoid problems or an unpleasant circumstance.

The trouble is, this nagging drives kids crazy and makes them resentful. After a while these parents encounter resistance and a variety of disagreeable reactions from their children, which is what they are trying to avoid in the first place. At some point kids start reacting to the nagging, either by arguing or by just ignoring their parents, because, as in the threatening style, kids quickly discover that there really are no teeth in the nagging.

Parents who nag need to confront their kids more directly, and let their children experience the consequences of their thoughtlessness, carelessness, or other negative behavior. And they need to be willing to administer consequences. Remind a child once, and then let life take its course. Parents have to be willing to let their children deal with the consequences, such as missing the car-pool ride to the swimming pool, and stop nagging them ten times for fear they'll lose out. The goal is to get the child to take responsibility for his or her life without constant reminders by the parent. Once the ride to the pool is missed, believe me, it won't happen again.

The Pleaser

Pleasers want their children to like them at all costs and at all times. Parents with this management style try to avoid confrontation and to make life easy for their kids—unfortunately, too easy. They usually make few demands on them. Kids who have a pleaser for a parent usually have few, if any, chores to do. The pleasing parent does almost everything around the house with little help from others. The whole family sits around after dinner watching TV, while "poor Mom" (it is usually Mom) clears the table, washes the dishes, sweeps the floor, and takes out the garbage. This is not a rare situation.

The pleaser has a habit of "asking" a child to do something, rather than commanding that it be done, and when the child says no, the parent is stuck:

> "April, will you take out the garbage for me, sweetheart?"
> "No, Mom, I'm too busy."

Parents who try too hard to please their children end up giving up too much power to them. What does this parent do when

April says she is too busy to take out the garbage? She might plead, "April, please take out the garbage for me." Or, "April, why can't you do what I'm asking? It's not that much." All too often Mom ends up doing it herself and ultimately resenting having to do everything.

Pleasers need to be willing to let their kids be upset with them from time to time. They need to let their kids be angry and even tell them that they don't like them. They also need to be sure that their kids have chores that are commensurate with their age. When they want something done, they need to use their authority with their kids, rather than asking, pleading, or begging. They need to take charge and trust that their kids will love them. Of course their kids will love them. Even when kids don't like their parents, they love them. If you find that you are a pleasing parent, take your power back.

The Boss

I have already said that you must be in charge, you must be the boss. So why, you ask, is the boss here as one of the undesirable styles? Because while you need to be in charge, and in that sense be the boss, you do not want to be controlling and authoritarian. You want to be the boss, but not bossy. So when I say the boss, I mean parents who order their kids around too much, who constantly tell them what to do and how to do it. Children in these families are not given many choices.

After she had realized that she was too bossy with her eight-year-old, one parent told me that she also noticed that she didn't listen to him very well. She realized that she was not giving him a sufficient chance to express his viewpoints and to disagree with her. Her son had begun to withdraw from her, and their relationship was strained.

This mother made two adjustments in her style. First, instead of ordering him around she gave him more choices during the disciplinary process. "When do you want to tidy up your room, before or after dinner?" Second, she really began listening to him in general. She took the time to find out what he thought about things. Their relationship soon shifted, almost dramatically. Not only did he become more cooperative, but they became much closer.

The Enforcer

A variation on the boss is the enforcer, who believes in force as a means to control kids. Force, however, tends to intimidate. Yelling, threats, and excessive punishment create too much fear in children. The message is: "I'm bigger than you, so you have to do what I say." In the dark ages of child rearing, the rationale was that if kids are scared, they will obey and be cooperative.

Although this style will work, at least for a while, it comes with a big price tag. Kids can become too scared. They can feel insecure. They can become timid. They can lack self-confidence. They can shut themselves down and hold back from initiating and exploring. Sometimes they react not only with fear, but they become angry and rebellious.

You do not have to be bossy or intimidating to manage kids. In relationships, force is not really power. Parental power stems not from being bigger or stronger, but from the fact that because you are the parent, you can control and impose consequences on a child's behavior. We'll see more about this in the next two chapters.

The Martyr

The martyr uses an ancient and revered approach to child management, one that is often handed down from generation to generation, and one that packs a wallop—guilt. The idea is that if you make children feel guilty, they will do what you want. Certainly you need to teach your children what is right and what is wrong; but you don't want to make them feel excessive guilt, and you definitely do not want to make them feel guilty in their relationship with you.

However, by making a child feel responsible for the parent's feelings in some way, the martyr approach does just that. "When you don't do your homework, it really hurts my feelings." "That makes it real hard for me." "How could you do that?"—accompanied by a few tears. And, of course, the classic, "Your Mother and I have done so much for you; how could you treat us like this!"

With this approach, children internalize the guilt and eventually end up feeling too much responsibility for others. This in turn can make them fearful of doing the "wrong thing," and they can end up being too passive. Moreover, this approach can generate a lot of resentment. Just as "where there is smoke there is fire," where there is excessive guilt there is resentment. And you don't want your kids resenting you.

Don't use guilt to motivate your kids. It is just not necessary. Use the tools that you will be given in the next few chapters, and you'll be far more successful.

The Critic

Every child must learn what behavior is acceptable and what is not acceptable. As a parent you must guide, correct, and steer your child in the right direction. You have to give your children feedback and guidance about their behavior. *How* you deliver this feedback, however, is incredibly important. It is critical that you not be critical.

There are various ways to end up being too critical. For example, parents can be too picky and exacting, requiring that every little detail be done just right. While any given critique may not be important, if this is a style, then the sheer weight of such critiques can be overwhelming to children, and they can end up feeling bad about themselves. They can feel like they can't do anything right and, therefore, are not good enough. This is hazardous to their self-esteem. They may also end up with the feeling that since they can't do anything right anyway, there's nothing to be gained by trying.

Another problem comes about when criticism turns into blame. When we get upset, it's quite easy to blame and label: "You're lazy." "You're slow." "Can't you do anything right?" But in the child's mind, it all comes down to a single message: "I can't do anything right."

Some think that faulting another motivates that person to change. Back in those dark ages of childrearing, people apparently thought that blaming and finding fault would motivate children to cooperate. Occasionally it does, but most of the time it simply makes kids feel bad about themselves.

Too much criticism can also make a child feel ashamed, and a little shame goes a long way on an emotional level. Shame is a feeling inside a person that says, "I am not as good as everyone else, and therefore I must hide." Shame can create fear of other people, a sense that "I don't want to be seen." Avoid using it to motivate your child.

Of course, you need to point out to your children when their behavior is unacceptable. But, it's a matter of *how* you tell them. You can tell them when they're wrong without making them wrong. You give them feedback about their behavior, not about who they are.

Try not to be picky or to label or to blame or to shame. Never bring the self-worth of your child into question. Deal with the behavior. It is the behavior that is not acceptable, not the child. Be sure your child knows that. Doing everything they can to foster their children's sense of self-esteem, self-worth, and self-love should be a sacred goal for all parents.

The Professor

This parent belongs to the academic school of child management. He—I hate to say this to you men, but it's usually the Father—believes that if you reason with children and offer explanations, sometimes detailed explanations, they will see the light. They will understand so well that they will be cooperative. To belong to this school of child management, you must possess a thorough and well-documented dossier of lectures that can be pulled out to deal with the issue of the moment.

"Martin," says his father, "you know you have to do your homework. You have to think about your future. If you don't do your work now and build good study habits, you may not get into college. Then what will you do? Tell me, Martin, what will happen if you don't get into college?"

"I dunno," replies Martin, glassy-eyed.

"You won't have a career, son. You won't get the things you want in life. You may not have a house like we have. You've got to do your homework, Martin, if you want to succeed."

Martin is nine.

Obviously, Martin's father wants the best for him. He wants him to succeed. Typically, parents who lecture and reason with their children think that nothing more is required. They think that reasoning alone will bring about the desired result, and they don't understand it when they have problems with discipline. Words, however, unless they are backed up by consistent action, such as parents spending some time helping with homework, are destined to fall on deaf ears.

I tell these parents not to talk so much. Keep explanations simple, brief, and at the child's level. Explain the rules and the consequences, but don't use language to manage your child. Moreover, don't try to convince them or persuade them. It's a waste of time, because kids have their own agenda. What helps them to accept your limits is the action you take, not your words.

I constantly encourage parents to look at their styles of managing and relating to their children. In fact, when there are problems, this is the first thing I suggest. And it is useful to check out your management style even if you are not having problems. An ounce of prevention goes a long way when it comes to relationships.

The first step I recommend is to step back and watch yourself as you manage and relate to your kids. If you see a problem, put things in slow motion in your mind and replay it. Since styles are so automatic and habitual, you may have to do this several times until you can see yourself clearly. Then notice the impact of your style. How does it affect your child? The parent who was too bossy did this and noticed that her child was resentful. A pleasing parent may notice that his or her child doesn't listen or just does whatever he wants.

If you suspect a problem and want to find out more about your style, ask those around you, your spouse, or friends. Then be open to their feedback. Just take it in. If it fits, do something about it, and if it doesn't, let it go.

Keep in mind that changing styles isn't easy. It takes attention and practice. You must be patient and understanding of yourself. You have to notice a style first; then you can change it. Just keep plugging away at it, and you can create an effective style.

Develop an Effective Parenting Style

1. Become aware of your current style by observing yourself and asking for feedback from others.

2. Assess the effectiveness of your style. Simply notice the results you are getting.

3. Eliminate the ineffective parts of your style.

4. Practice the firm, gentle approach.

PARENTS HAVE BUTTONS, TOO

Everyone reacts emotionally to life's events. You get caught in a traffic jam on the way to the airport, and you feel anxious and angry. You experience a loss in the stock market, and you feel depressed. A relative becomes seriously ill, and you feel sad. A friend cancels a social engagement, and you feel disappointed. These spontaneous reactions are all natural and a part of life with which we are all too familiar.

Your kids are going to upset you, too. Even though you love your children dearly, they can and will push your buttons. One parent told me that her four-year-old's whining can grate like fingernails on a blackboard, and it is all she can do not to scream at times. Another parent reported how when he has to ask his nine-year-old five or six times to pick up his books, clothes, and toys that lie scattered around the house, he finds himself starting to smolder. Still another set of parents recounted that outright defiance from their ten-year-old makes them feel utterly helpless. They said it is as though they are paralyzed.

All of these reactions are natural and a part of life. However, if certain emotional reactions become automatic and ongoing, that is, if we have difficulty managing our feelings, they can interfere with discipline and cause our management style to become ineffective. In the spirit of stepping back to put your life with kids in slow motion and to look objectively at what goes on, ask yourself whether there are any ongoing patterns to your own reactions that interfere with your ability to discipline effectively. Here is an example of one such situation.

Charles was a single parent who came to see me about his son Terry, who was nine and becoming out of control. Terry not only was disobedient but also was surly, argumentative, and demanding. At one point, Charles told me the following:

"Recently when I told him to clean his room, he said to me, 'I don't want to. Why should I? I don't have to do what you say. I'll clean it when I feel like it.' And he threw his book down. I couldn't believe it—that he would talk to me in that defiant, surly tone—but then I realized that he had been talking to me in a very similar way for some time."

"How did you handle it, Charles?" I asked.

"I was really mad. I wanted to send him to his room for a week."

"What did you do?"

"I yelled at him. I told him to go to his room and not come out until I told him he could."

Charles thought for a moment and then said: "You know, I'm realizing something here. Every time he defies me—and he's been doing it for a while now—I get upset like this. I mean I *feel* really upset. I do yell at him quite a bit. His defiance really gets to me. Now that we're talking about it, I think I take it real personally. As though he doesn't like me."

Charles was beginning to understand that he had a hot button. Whenever his son talked to him in a surly, argumentative, or defiant way, he became angry. And it made it difficult for him to deal with Terry in a fair, consistent, and effective manner.

This doesn't mean Charles was a bad parent. In fact, he was actually a very good parent, but this one area was difficult for him. It confused him, and he really did not know how to handle his response to his son. He was inconsistent and ineffective, and his yelling made the situation worse. Most people have areas like this in their lives that bring up emotional responses and that make some aspect of dealing with others difficult. As parents, almost all of us have some buttons in response to our children's behavior, and it is important to be willing to look at ourselves. We are only human and, therefore, should face ourselves without incrimination. Looking at ourselves can make us uncomfortable; but it is worth it, especially when it comes to our kids.

What do you do when you find that you have a button that is interfering with disciplining effectively? The most important thing is to take responsibility for it. In other words, own your reaction. Other people do not *cause* our emotional reactions. They may trigger them, but we create them. Contrary to how it may seem sometimes, nobody, not even our own kids, can make us feel what we feel. The actions or words of others connect to something in us that is sensitive, and then we react.

In Charles's case, he thought that his son didn't like him. This was the button. Terry's defiance triggered a deeper reaction in Charles that made him feel very badly inside himself. The problem was that it came out as anger, and his anger made the problem worse. When Charles realized where his anger was actually coming from, he was able to manage it better, and eventually began to see that Terry's defiance really had nothing to do with liking him. That defused his anger, and he was able to let go of it and, as a result, manage Terry more effectively. He soon no longer felt that Terry was causing him to be angry.

In addition, parents get angry when they don't know what to do in certain situations requiring discipline. They feel helpless. Because they feel like they have lost control, they believe they must resort to more forceful methods, like yelling or threats. In some situations, it is hard to know what to do. Often it is best to do nothing rather than take just any kind of action. Take the time to think the situation through and consult others.

If you feel angry, take responsibility for it. Don't blame your child. Take a little deeper look inside to see where it is coming from. And be patient. It won't necessarily go away right away.

Another emotional button that can get in the way of setting limits and employing consequences is too readily feeling the pain of others. Some parents can't stand to see their children suffer. When they have to inflict pain on their child, withdrawing a privilege, for example, they feel anguished and often guilty. Their solution is to hold back the consequence. If this becomes a pattern, their undisciplined kids soon become resistive, unruly, and demanding, because there haven't been consequences linked to their misbehavior. And then they end up with bigger problems. You need to be able to let kids feel hurt sometimes. It is not that you want to hurt them; but you must help them learn their lessons, and sometimes that is painful for them.

If you find that you hold back or are reluctant to apply consequences, ask yourself if you are reluctant to have other people feel hurt. Then think about the worst thing that could happen if, for example, your child didn't get to go to the movies because he had neglected his chores. If you think it through, you'll be able to see that nothing terrible will happen. Then you won't hold back from administering consequences.

SOME ENCOURAGEMENT

This chapter focused on certain aspects of parenting—styles and emotional reactions. These issues are not easy to confront in ourselves. Yet, these areas are crucial to the success of discipline and a good relationship between parents and children.

No one likes to discover things about himself or herself that may need changing or adjusting. Most of us are a little sensitive to this. Yet, we need to be honest with ourselves. Know that you are doing your best—you wouldn't be reading this book if you weren't. You are putting the well-being of your children first. If in the process of reading this chapter, you discovered you have made some mistakes, don't feel bad about yourself and don't devalue your worth as a parent. You're only human. A better measure of your worth is the ability to change, to correct your course. That's the real measure of a good parent, and that's really what you are doing by reading this book.

CHAPTER TWO

How Do Your Kids Talk to You?

*C*hildren do not come into this world prepackaged to be obedient and cooperative. At times, they outright refuse to do what you ask; at other times, they say they will comply but don't. Sometimes they just dawdle. Sometimes they lose little "unimportant" things like their schoolbooks, their jackets, or their shoes. As psychologists are wont to say, "Raising children ain't easy."

MISBEHAVIOR AND THE WAYS KIDS TALK

When children are misbehaving, are hard to manage, or are just plain uncooperative, they always find ways to resist you. Sometimes it seems that a misbehaving child's sole mission in life is to fight you tooth and nail. (If only they had a mission to do their homework or clean their room!) The problem isn't simply that they misbehave or are uncooperative; it is also that they resist.

Resistance shows up mainly in the way kids talk and relate. When kids misbehave, they tend to be disrespectful to their parents and sometimes to other adults as well. They're rude, sassy, and discourteous. They talk back, whine, argue, defy, are demanding, and so forth. They don't just resist with their behavior, they resist with their mouths. Here are some other ways that kids resist their parents:

Your four-year-old whines at you all day long in that high-pitched, nasal tone of voice that makes you want to forget family life and head for the Caribbean. You try, but you just can't get him to talk in a normal tone of voice.

When you ask your six-year-old to pick up his toys, which are scattered throughout the house, he moans and groans, as though the world were coming to an end. "Why do *I* have to pick them up?" he complains. "Eric never has to. You never make him do anything. I always have to do everything." It takes nearly ten minutes for you to get him to pick up his toys. It's gotten to the point that you hate to give him a chore because you don't want to listen to his incessant complaining.

Your seven-year-old wants to spend the night at her friend's, but you tell her no. She nags you about it off and on all evening long. "Why can't I go to Julie's? I don't have school tomorrow." And later, "Please, please, Mom, can I go to Julie's?" Eventually she tries Dad: "PLEASE, Dad, can I spend the night at Julie's?" You both are relieved when bedtime rolls around and you can get her out of your hair.

It's nearly six o'clock, and you tell your eight-year-old to finish his homework. It's just a simple request. "I DON'T WANT TO," he screams. "I'M SICK OF HOMEWORK!" He throws his pencil and stomps off.

Your ten-year-old wants the latest CD that all the kids are buying. She demands that you drop everything and take her to the store right away. "Mom, you've got to take me down to the mall. I have to get this CD." When you refuse, she says, "Mom, *everybody* has this CD. I have to get one today." When you still don't yield, she goes to her room and slams the door.

These children are all relating negatively to their parents. In one way or another they are being rude, sassy, and disrespectful:

The four-year-old whines.
The six-year-old complains.
The seven-year-old nags.
The eight-year-old screams.
The ten-year-old demands.

The whining, nagging, screaming, demanding, and complaining are negative and oppositional ways of relating. These behaviors are what we actually encounter when we say children are disrespectful. To be effective at discipline, we must be able to deal with the negative and oppositional way our kids talk to us.

Here are the most common negative and oppositional ways of relating that I have noticed that children engage in:

whining	bossing	yelling
complaining	demanding	screaming
nagging	threatening	throwing tantrums
arguing	talking back	defying
pleading	antagonizing	being belligerent

If your child is misbehaving, then you have run into some of these behaviors. While your child probably does not exhibit all of these behaviors, there is probably some combination of them that is unique to him or her.

You've heard the expression "Don't give me any flak." That is how one parent told me that she experiences her child's way of talking to her. "It explodes all around me," she explained. "And I can't get him to do what I ask. It throws me off and it wears me down. Often, I just give up."

Sometimes being a parent does feel like you are caught in a barrage of enemy antiaircraft fire. And your mission—let's say to get the toys in the living room put away—suddenly seems daunting, even dangerous. While flak from your children may not actually be life threatening, it certainly can be stressful and hard on your mental health, especially if it persists. Moreover, it interferes with discipline and setting limits.

Misbehaving kids resist their parents by talking and relating in oppositional ways. If parents know how to manage and deal with these ways of relating, children won't be able to resist as much; and if they don't resist as much, they won't misbehave nearly as much.

It's really very simple. But simple does not mean easy.

NEGATIVE WAYS OF TALKING VERSUS MISBEHAVIOR

Because it is important that you are completely clear about the difference between a negative style and misbehavior, here is a list that contrasts the two:

Misbehaviors	*Oppositional Styles*
disobeying	whining
ignoring	complaining
taking others' possessions	defying
fighting	arguing
not doing chores	yelling
not doing homework	demanding
running away	screaming
dawdling	throwing tantrums
not coming home on time	talking back
lying	nagging

This is not an exhaustive list of misbehaviors and oppositional styles by any means, but it should give you a good idea of the differences between a misbehavior and a negative style. Misbehavior is any behavior that does not conform to rules and responsibilities that have been established. A resistive style, on the other hand, is the verbal and nonverbal way a child expresses himself or herself in a given interaction. When children relate appropriately and the negative ways of talking and verbally resisting are minimal, discipline becomes much smoother.

When the Usual Resistance Becomes an Oppositional Style

Most kids will talk back, whine, and argue with you from time to time. This is only natural and normal. However, you don't want children to develop oppositional styles of relating to you. You don't want the occasional back talk or whining to become habitual and automatic. When kids are difficult to manage, however, that is exactly what happens. They fall into habitual negative and oppositional ways of relating to you and responding to the limits you set.

Parents whose kids are cooperative and easy to manage do not allow their kids to talk to them in negative ways. On the other hand, parents who are having difficulty managing their kids often do not realize the importance of how a child talks and relates to them during discipline; they allow their children to relate and respond in oppositional ways. They usually overlook the oppositional style or try to work around it.

The most effective way to deal with misbehavior is to know how to manage any oppositional style of relating that a child has, and the most effective way to discipline is not to allow such styles to develop in the first place.

Once you understand how important it is to manage your child's negative and oppositional styles, you have a key tool to manage your child effectively. If your children *relate* to you respectfully, if their styles are not consistently resistive, you won't have any major problems with discipline. Follow the suggestions below to become more knowledgeable about your child's style.

Familiarize Yourself with Your Child's Style

1. Observe your children's style. Just watch for a while to see how they relate to you. (Refer back to the list of misbehaviors and oppositional styles.)

2. Be sure to distinguish between the style and any misbehaviors.

3. Make a list of these styles.

4. Notice the situations in which these styles occur.

DISCIPLINE

What is discipline? Basically, it is nothing more than telling your child no. Sometimes it may involve a physical act, such as grabbing your small child as he races headlong toward the street. Sometimes it involves approved choices for play, such as directing your child toward building with an erector set, rather than the power tools in the basement. And sometimes it involves setting limits on activities, such as telling your six-year-old that she can go to her friend's house down the street, but that she can't go around the corner.

Why is discipline so difficult? Why can't kids just do what they're told so that everyone can live happily ever after? There are many reasons for this, but three are particularly important. One reason is that it is not always easy for parents to know what the standards are for a given age. How much responsibility to give a child, how much freedom, and what the rules should be are all questions that are bound to challenge you. Since it is impossible always to know exactly what expectations are reasonable, all parents are bound to be inconsistent at times, and this creates confusion for kids.

Another reason why discipline is so difficult is that much of it is spontaneous. You have to think on your feet. On any given day, you may have to decide whether to grant a new freedom, like allowing your ten-year-old to cross a busy street on her bicycle to visit her new best friend; or you may have to handle a conflict between two of your kids, who have managed to break each other's toys; or you may have to deal with the mess that your four-year-old made in the garage. No one said it was going to be easy.

The third and most important reason is that limit setting is an emotionally loaded situation. Children often react when you set limits on them. They want what they want when they want it, and they can become dramatically upset at times when they don't get their wishes and demands met. This, in turn, can be upsetting for you.

Unfortunately, even effective discipline and limit-setting techniques can create situations that are tailor-made for conflict and upset. In most families, there is probably more upset around discipline than around anything else. In order to discipline effectively, you need to know how to manage and deal with the conflicts and upsets that can occur so often in the course of the disciplinary process, and that, of course, involves relating.

DISCIPLINE AND HOW YOU RELATE

Discipline is not a silent affair. It requires that you and your child talk and relate to each other. You relate when you communicate about rules and consequences, you relate when you handle spontaneous problems as they arise, and you relate when you deal with your kids when they become upset about restrictions that you place on them. How you and your child relate during the disciplinary process is a crucial part of discipline.

If the relating and interacting go poorly during limit setting so that upsets occur, two things can happen. The first is that the outcome of discipline will be affected. The upset and unhappy feelings will get in the way, making it more difficult to manage the situation. Second, the overall relationship between parent and child will suffer. (This is particularly true when the interactions around discipline consistently go poorly.) Angry and hurt feelings can linger and create distance in the relationship. We can diagram it this way:

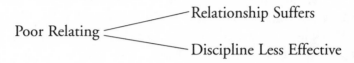

Over time, poor relating around discipline issues undermines your authority and creates resistance in children. At first, you may not notice it. Then, all of a sudden, you have a major problem on your hands, like a child acting up in school. But these problems are not sudden; they build up. If you know what to look for, you can prevent them.

On the other hand, if you and your child relate positively and constructively during discipline, just the opposite happens. Your relationship will be good and discipline will go well. You and your child will feel close to each other. Conflicts will be resolved more easily, and there will be far fewer upsets. Now, we can diagram it this way:

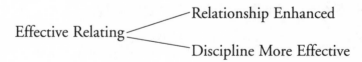

To say it succinctly, *discipline will be successful only when the relating and interacting that occur around it are constructive.* Moreover, when the relating during discipline is positive and constructive, your overall relationship with your children will be positively affected.

Since managing children is a big part of family life, discipline has a huge emotional impact on the family. Just about the most important thing to children is to feel close to their parents. When you and your kids relate well on a day-to-day basis, especially around the many discipline issues that naturally come up in the course of living, your relationship will flourish, your children will feel close to you, and discipline will become relatively easy; believe it or not, they will *want* to cooperate with you and to please you.

THE CARDINAL RULE

Alan won't come when he is called.
Kim doesn't do her homework.
Derrick is constantly late.
Jonathan won't put his toys away.
Allison won't clean her room.
Stacy won't get ready for school in the morning.

Where do you start when your children are disobedient and won't cooperate?

Here is the cardinal rule:

To manage misbehavior, first correct any oppositional style that is present.

Misbehavior does not occur without some spoken resistance on the part of the child. When you encounter misbehavior, don't ignore it and don't go around it. Address the child's resistance, that is, his or her style of relating in that moment. (Part Two gives some powerful strategies to assist you.)

Because we all want misbehavior to go away, we tend to address that first; that is most important to us at that moment. However, make an adjustment; correct the oppositional style first. Then deal with the specific misbehavior.

If you are struggling with your child, make a card with the cardinal rule on it, and put it on your bathroom mirror or your refrigerator as a constant reminder to you. That's how important it is!

If you have a child who is very disobedient, whose misbehavior is persistent and seems entrenched, the cardinal rule is all the more important. Don't even think about correcting the misbehavior until you deal with his or her oppositional style. (Chapter 14 addresses the difficult child.)

Nip Oppositional Styles in the Bud

When you encounter whining, arguing, or any negative style, don't let it pass by. Comment on it.

"It's not okay to argue with me."

"I don't like your tone of voice right now. Ask me nicely."

"You have to ask me if you want milk, not tell me. Now try that again."

OPPOSITIONAL STYLES AND KIDS' EMOTIONS

In order to manage your child's style effectively, there are two things you need to know. First, a child's oppositional style does not usually consist of just one behavior, such as whining, but is usually composed of a variety of behaviors. One child may be whiny, bossy, and have tantrums. Another may be argumentative and antagonistic. And still another child may be demanding, defiant, and belligerent. Kids who are misbehaving, then, have oppositional styles that are a combination of several behaviors.

Second, these different styles vary in their emotional intensity. Sometimes kids are just a little upset, sometimes a lot. A child's nagging, for example, while annoying, has less emotion in it than defiance or screaming, which can make you feel quite overwhelmed—even scared or angry—when directed at you.

Understanding the different levels of upset will help you deal with oppositional styles more effectively. I have found it useful to group kids' negative styles into four categories, according to how emotionally intense they are. From the list of the most common oppositional styles from earlier in this chapter, here are the categories from the least to the most intense:

Level one: whining, complaining, nagging
Level two: arguing, pleading, talking back, bossing
Level three: defying, threatening, demanding, yelling, antagonizing, being belligerent

Level four: screaming, throwing tantrums (including throwing things, slamming doors, and running away while being corrected)

The more emotionally intense a child's style is, the more difficult it will be to handle a child in a given situation. A level-one behavior, such as complaining, is easier to handle than a level-four behavior, such as throwing tantrums, although I am not saying that a whining style is necessarily easy to handle. Furthermore, the more intense styles have more impact on whomever the child is interacting with. Most of the time, you will feel your child's temper tantrum, a level-four behavior, much more strongly than something like bossiness, a level-two behavior. This can result in your feeling embarrassed (especially if you're in public), uneasy (because the situation is out of your control), furious (because your adrenalin is pumping), or all of the above.

When kids are difficult to manage, you will encounter level-three and level-four behaviors frequently. These behaviors are hard to ignore. You can't just walk away from them or let them go. The very intensity of these encounters demands a lot of you as a parent. Disobedient and hard-to-manage kids are more reactive and, therefore, much more taxing on your time, energy, and patience. They are, in fact, so demanding that when parents finally do get on top of that kind of behavior, they often feel, "At last I've got my own life back!"

Let's suppose that in addition to being disobedient, a child is defiant and belligerent, and has temper tantrums. You can tear your hair out trying to deal with these very intense ways of relating. Anne described to me how her eight-year-old reacts to discipline: "I ask him to do something, like take out the garbage, and right away he raises his voice and sometimes even yells, 'No, I don't want to,' or 'I don't have to. You can't make me.'"

This type of situation is just inches from exploding into a major power struggle—or maybe even a war. These kinds of reactions and defiance can paralyze you. What do you do? What is the best way to handle this situation? How do you deal with the strongly charged and oppositional reactions in your child?

THE SECRET TO MANAGING YOUR CHILD'S STYLE

Children who are regularly operating at levels three and four with styles that are defiant and belligerent, and with frequent temper tantrums, also manifest behaviors at levels one and two. Moreover, in the great majority of situations, the oppositional styles at levels one and two occur much more frequently than those at levels three and four. We don't tend to focus on these less intense styles, because the more intense ones impact us much more powerfully, demanding our attention, not to mention trying our patience.

The bright side of all of this is that the less intense styles are much easier to deal with than the more intense ones. They give you an opening for beginning the process of helping your child to develop more positive and, ultimately, more rewarding styles. It takes far less energy to gain control over a child's whining than a child's defiance. The reason is simple, though often overlooked: The child is more in control emotionally. Here is the secret to managing a child's negative style:

Deal with the least intense aspects of your child's style first.

Don't try to change your child's tantrums or defiance right away. Save those behaviors for later. Start the change process at the point of least resistance. Though it might seem like an obvious place to start, this fact often gets missed. We overlook it because with a child who is also manifesting intense higher level oppositional styles, we get into the habit of ignoring level one and two styles. Likewise, many parents fear addressing the lower level behaviors because they might escalate into the higher level behaviors.

When you find that your child has a negative style, begin by observing him or her closely with the goal of identifying all of the behaviors that make up the negative style. Then sort the styles into the four levels. This will give you an idea of the range and intensity of your child's negative style and of where you are likely to be most successful in your efforts to make positive changes.

As you begin focusing your attention on the less intense emotional reactions, mainly the behaviors at levels one and two, you will generally find that they occur much more frequently than the more intense ones. This is the silver lining. Since they occur more frequently than the behaviors at levels three and four, you naturally have more opportunities for making the kind of changes you want at the least intense level of how your child relates to you.

Suppose that you have observed your child's overall behavior and have noted that he argues a lot more than he yells and screams. (The main exception will be the child who has an attention deficit disorder.) Although our tendency is to gloss over the lower level behavior—the arguing—and to get literally pulled into the more negative reactions, especially when they have escalated to the point where they are out of control, or nearly so, we should do just the opposite, that is, address the lower level behavior.

Jason was nearly six when his parents consulted me about his tantrums:

> "He's unruly," explained Jan. "He only obeys me when he feels like it, and that isn't very often."
>
> "It's his temper tantrums that get to me," said Chuck. "He'll throw a fit at the drop of a hat. We're walking on eggs all the time, trying not to upset him."
>
> "I feel terrible," lamented Jan with tears in her eyes. "It seems like we're constantly at odds. And it's affecting Sarah, our three-year-old. She is starting to get very upset when Jason gets mad."

Here was a child who misbehaved and had tantrums, a level-four style, one that is the extreme of emotional intensity. After discussing the tantrums in depth with Jason's parents, I inquired about how he interacted with them in general. Did he whine, argue, nag, or make demands on them? They were not sure. They thought he might argue sometimes and perhaps whine a bit.

At the end of our first meeting, I asked them to observe his style as he interacted with them and to note whether he had any other oppositional ways of responding to them besides the tantrums. I suggested that they write down some examples, if they found any (I was pretty sure they would), and asked them to keep a rough count.

When they came back the following week, they were amazed by what they had discovered:

> "He whines all the time," said Jan. "I never realized it."
>
> "Did you keep a count?" I asked.
>
> "Yes," she replied. "I couldn't believe it the first day I did it. He whined nine times. And that's very typical. I guess I have gotten used to it, but each day as I tracked his whining I became more upset. The worst was the day he whined sixteen times. I was very irritated with him."

Jason's whining was clearly out of control.

Jan and Chuck's situation is not unusual. It is so easy to overlook whining and similar behaviors in a child's style. But these behaviors can occur constantly, creating many minor disruptions during the day. As a result, they end up being just as disruptive as tantrums, if not more so.

Just knowing how frequently a behavior like whining occurs can make a major difference in your perception of the problem. When I suggested that we start helping Jason by dealing with his whining first, Jan and Chuck were more than willing to do so because once they recognized how extensive it was, they also realized that they were quite tired of it. And they felt badly about it. They did not want to feel irritated and upset with Jason so often about his behavior.

"Don't worry about the tantrums," I told them. "For now just ignore them the best you can. They will get better when you change his whining." Although they were not so sure about this statement, we set up a program to work on Jason's whining (which we'll explore in the next section).

In adults, unwanted or negative interpersonal styles are difficult to change. They become ingrained over the years. While styles are also difficult to change in children, they are not as fixed. Unlike adults, children are much more flexible and open to change, particularly when they experience benefits from doing so. If you understand what makes a style tick and you know how to approach it in a systematic way, you will find to your surprise and relief that you *can* manage and change it, often with far less energy than you might have supposed.

CHANGING THE WHINING CHANGES THE TANTRUMS

Before we continue with Jason, let's look at why I told his parents that the tantrums would get better when the whining got better. What does changing his whining have to do with changing his tantrums? Was it an idle boast on my part, or did I have a good reason to think this approach would work?

It is important to understand that the more emotionally intense the style is, the more a child is out of control. With level-four behaviors, the child is more out of control than at levels one, two, and three. As a child's controls diminish, your efforts to reach him or her become increasingly challenging.

All the oppositional behaviors that make up a style, however, are to some degree out of control. Emotional intensity is one way for styles to be out of control, but not the only way. The situation with Jason is not uncommon. Almost every day he has a tantrum and occasionally two or three, but also on a typical day he whines and nags his parents anywhere from five to ten times, and on some days it is considerably more than that. Clearly, his whining and nagging are out of control. It is not just his tantrums that are the problem.

Start Managing Oppositional Styles Now

1. Observe your child to find the least intense style.

2. Target that one for change. Do not start with tantrums.

3. For now, just say, "I won't talk to you when you use that tone of voice."

(More strategies are explained in Part Two.)

You should be aware that styles can be out of control in two ways: in their intensity and in their frequency. Consequently, all oppositional ways of relating that are habitual, even the less intense ones, reflect a problem with a child's self-control. Their high frequencies of occurrence make them out of control. When a child whines or argues or nags as much as Jason does, the child needs guidance to find control of his reactions. In a very real way, he has become a victim of his behavior as much as his parents have.

When you help children control a less intense style, like whining, this change affects *all* aspects of a child's style. Therefore, when a level-one style like whining either diminishes or goes away, after a while the more emotionally intense reactions like defiance and tantrums also begin to occur less often. That is because all styles of reacting and interacting are interrelated. To successfully change a behavior like whining is to give a child greater control of his or her life. All of a child's emotional reactions are affected. He or she becomes less reactive in general. In other words, it is like pulling out one of the blocks on the bottom of the pyramid. When you pull out a block, the whole pyramid is weakened. It begins to tilt to one side. When you pull out another, the whole pyramid is likely to collapse. The structure can't hold itself up.

The same thing is true with negative styles. The highly intense ones rest on the less emotionally intense ones. When you change or remove one of the less intense behaviors, then very intense reactions, like yelling and screaming, will soon start decreasing both in intensity and frequency. Sometimes they go away on their own, and you never even need to address them directly. Always they become much easier for you to manage.

This improved ability of the child to manage his or her emotional reactions and styles of relating also leads to a lessening of misbehavior. As with the styles, you may never need to address some of them directly. Less strife and conflict lead to a boost in good will and, as a result, cooperation.

When Jason's parents realized the extent of his whining, they were quite motivated to change it, even though they were skeptical that it would help his tantrums. Using some of the tools in the next two chapters, they put a plan in place to deal with his whining.

First, Jason's parents discovered that they were rewarding him for his whining. They found that they would listen to him while he whined and that they would try to stop the whining by giving in to him. (Rewarding misbehavior is discussed in more depth later.) Thus, they changed their response to it. They acknowledged him for talking appropriately to them, especially when they put limits on his behavior or refused him a request. For example, they would tell him that they appreciated his talking nicely to them or thank him for not whining. Within ten days, Jason's whining decreased dramatically, and his parents soon found that they were less frustrated with him and were enjoying being with him much more. Shortly thereafter, they noticed that his tantrums were decreasing in frequency and duration.

Next, they addressed his demanding behavior, which they had begun to notice more clearly as they were dealing with his whining. Jason would make statements such as this: "Take me over to Gary's (his friend). I have to see him right away." Using the same methods they used in dealing with his whining, Jason's parents were successful in dealing with this behavior, and they noticed that his tantrums decreased further. After three weeks, Jason's tantrums were occurring only once or twice a week, compared with once a day. Moreover, he had made significant improvement in following directions and obeying rules.

Jason and his parents then continued the program on their own. In a follow-up call several weeks later, they reported not only that he had stopped being so whiny and demanding but also that he had had only two tantrums in the intervening weeks, and even these did not last very long.

The following chart shows you how to look at the problems illustrated in the situation with Jason:

Concerns: disobedient; temper tantrums
Strategy: redefine the problem; focus on the whining, and then the demanding behavior (instead of the tantrums)
Results: tantrums almost completely gone; child cooperative

SUMMARY

The key to discipline is to make sure that your children talk and relate to you respectfully and appropriately. Do not allow normal verbal resistance to develop into oppositional styles. If they already have, then you need to help your child change these ways of relating. Children's oppositional ways of relating vary in their emotional intensity. When attempting to change a child's oppositional style, start with the least emotionally intense behavior in the style pattern. The less intense behaviors are easier to change, and when you successfully change any part of a child's style, then more intense stylistic behaviors lessen, and he or she becomes easier to manage in general. Less conflict and emotional upset lead to positive and constructive ways of relating, bringing parents and children closer together and motivating children to be obedient.

Make effective and constructive relating your first concern, whether you have discipline problems or not. If you and your child relate well around discipline, discipline will go well. Constructive relating defuses potential upsets and makes conflicts easier to resolve. It takes a big portion of the tension out of family living. Relate well, and life becomes more satisfying.

PART TWO

Tools for Setting Limits

*P*art Two focuses on specific tools and techniques to deal with various kinds of misbehavior. These tools will also enable you to prevent misbehavior in the first place.

Chapter Three shows how to set limits and boundaries—how to establish rules and responsibilities for children that are clear and appropriate. It also provides a variety of ways to communicate these limits and boundaries to your children.

Chapter Four explains how several different tools, such as logical and natural consequences, rewards, and modeling desired behavior, can be used to change both oppositional styles and misbehavior.

CHAPTER THREE

Establishing and Communicating Clear Limits and Boundaries

*Y*our nine-year-old wants to go to the mall after school with her friends. Do you let her?

Your six-year-old leaves her bike outside overnight. How do you handle it?

Your three-and-a-half-year-old wants to watch cartoons that contain violence. Should he be allowed to do this?

You face these and dozens of other decisions every day, all day long, requiring you to set limit after limit. This all too familiar and unrelenting process can be stressful, challenging, and even daunting at times. Yet, knowing how, when, and where to set limits is crucial to the successful disciplining and training of your child.

Children need a clearly defined space in which to operate. When you set limits, you define that space; and in so doing, you define the boundaries of your child's world. It is like building a room for them. You determine the size of that room and the placement of the walls. And you do that through the rules and expectations that you communicate to them.

The room you create for them could be the size of a cubicle, so small that there is hardly any room to maneuver. Too many rules and regulations would make this room so tiny that kids would have few choices and little freedom.

On the other hand, you could make the room huge. It could be the size of the Superdome. Imagine a four-year-old wandering around an empty Superdome. The child would be lost and undoubtedly frightened in such a huge space. In a room such as this, a child could not easily find the walls. There would not be enough rules and routines to provide the structure the child needs. Too many choices and too much freedom would make him or her feel insecure.

Children need a room that is not so small that they cannot explore, have choices, and make decisions, but not so large that they have too many choices and must make too many decisions. Kids need a structure that supports them, one that defines their world through reasonable rules and guidelines but at the same time gives them room to maneuver. "Too large" or "too small" can easily lead to a child who is insecure.

The first step in setting limits, then, is to have clearly defined boundaries for your children to operate in. These boundaries are set up by your expectations. These are the rules and routines that you make for them, and the chores and tasks that you assign them. Think through your expectations deliberately and carefully so that you can set appropriate and effective limits. While you cannot anticipate all the situations that will come up, this advance planning should enable you to be far more clear and consistent than you would be otherwise.

But there is more to it. A child's behavior is bounded on the one side by your expectations for their behavior and on the other by the consequences for their behavior. These "bookends" look like this:

Expectations—Behavior—Consequences

The consequences encourage the child to comply to our expectations. In order to set limits effectively, you need expectations to outline the boundaries of your child's world and consequences to keep these boundaries intact. Expectations are communicated primarily through rules and responsibilities, which is the focus of this chapter. (Chapter Four explores in detail how to use consequences.)

R AND R FOR KIDS

Adults aren't the only ones who need a little R and R. Kids need some too. But sorry, kids, I'm not telling your parents to take you to Hawaii. In this book R and R means rules and responsibilities. Children need R and R to grow into mature adults. Rules and responsibilities provide direction for children and direction for parents, too, because they provide a context from which to manage children. One of the most common routes to an uncooperative child is for parents to require little or nothing from the child. Ask yourself what kind of rules and responsibilities you want for your children and what you want these to accomplish.

RULES

Rules are a guide for conduct. They create order and help life to flow more smoothly. They provide bearings in life so that the destination can be reached. The destination here is adulthood. Since kids internalize this order, they can eventually run their lives in a self-directed and consistent fashion.

What happens when there is a scarcity of rules? It's chaos time on the old ranchero. Since kids don't know what is required, and there are few demands placed on them; they just do whatever they want. They leave things lying around, they wander off, and they come home when they feel like it. Sometimes they make their beds; sometimes they don't.

After a while, these kids expect life to be easy. They don't want to be bothered or inconvenienced. A chore taking more than five minutes, then two minutes, and finally one minute becomes a monumental hardship. They want what they want—now.

When their parents try to introduce rules, they run into resistance. In fact, they are likely to run into a lot more than resistance. Kids raised with few rules rebel and become difficult to manage. Mom and Dad become unhappy, and they don't understand why the kids are so difficult. The kids often talk disrespectfully to them because there are no rules about that either.

It is not easy to set rules. You have to determine, for example, the following: How far can your five-year-old go from the house? How soon should your eight-year-old be home after school? How much running around do you allow in the house? How much TV and which programs can the kids watch? What time does your five-year-old or your eleven-year-old go to bed?

Unfortunately, there are no hard-and-fast answers to most of these questions. The answers vary from family to family. You have to decide for yourself. I certainly would not presume to tell you. It's a matter of lifestyle, taste, personality, values, and comfort levels.

Whatever you decide, rules and responsibilities need to be reasonable and age appropriate, and you must be consistent. If you are not sure what constitutes reasonable and appropriate, talk to other parents, a teacher, or your pediatrician. Or head to the library; there are scores of books that can help you understand what kids can do at each developmental stage.

When parents are divorced, it is important that they have similar rules. You don't want children going from a permissive environment to an authoritarian one, for example. It is confusing for them, and it can set up unnecessary conflicts. Parents must set aside their differences for the good of their children.

RESPONSIBILITIES

Every child needs to have some responsibilities. A two-and-a-half-year-old can help put the scattered toys into the toy box; at the more advanced age of four he does this by himself. A seven-year-old can set the table for dinner each evening; a ten-year-old can bring in the garbage cans; and a twelve-year-old can vacuum and dust. Most responsibilities consist of chores and tasks that help the family function. Make a list of each child's chores and put it in a prominent place, like on the refrigerator door.

At every developmental level, having chores and responsibilities gives children the opportunity to contribute to the family. The older they grow, the more privileges they receive, and the more responsibilities they assume. Kids need to learn that privileges and responsibilities go together.

Arnold and Christine consulted me about their daughter Andrea. Eight-year-old Andrea had become surly and argumentative. "Suddenly" she was becoming a problem. On the few occasions she was asked to do a chore, she refused. Andrea said, "I'm too busy. I want to be with my friends." In school she was becoming disruptive in class and was not doing her homework.

Andrea's parents had never required her to contribute to the family. They had never assigned her regular chores to do. They had never established any daily and weekly responsibilities for her to handle. Throughout her growing up, her mother had only occasionally asked her to help.

Andrea felt she should be able to do whatever she wanted. Arnold and Christine said that it seemed all they ever heard from her was "I want—I want—I want." The problems came to a head when Arnold and Christine discovered that she had been sneaking out of the neighborhood to play with some older children a few streets away. Moreover, these were children that Arnold and Christine thought could be a bad influence on their daughter.

Her parents told her that she would be on restriction, and Andrea rebelled. The next day she sneaked out of the house very early. Arnold and Christine were frantic and on the verge of calling the police to report her missing when they found her at about eleven o'clock in a group of those same kids a few blocks away.

Andrea had not been provided with enough responsibilities and, therefore, boundaries. Now she needed them, and this produced quite a challenge for Andrea's parents. It took a great deal of effort and perseverance for them to deal with Andrea's resistance before she became cooperative. They had to deal with her surly and argumentative style first (the cardinal rule). Then, they gradually introduced chores and responsibilities with appropriate consequences. Little by little, Andrea came to accept that she had a part to play in the family. And you can't blame Andrea. She had never been required to look beyond herself.

Andrea had two younger sisters, ages six and five. They too had never been assigned chores and responsibilities. Needless to say, the parents immediately remedied that, before any major problems developed with them.

Involve Andrea in the Family

Goal: to have Andrea become responsible and a participating member of the family

New Requirements for Andrea:

1. Daily chores: to set the table each evening and to feed the cat

2. Weekly chores: to clean her room and to dust the living room

3. A special "chore" (that her parents thought Andrea actually would enjoy): to help her mother make up the weekly food shopping list

ACCOUNTABILITY

Limit setting teaches children to be accountable for their actions, and accountability is the cornerstone of responsibility. Having rules to follow and chores to do means that children must at some point and in some way give a reckoning for their behavior. Your expectations on the one side and consequences on the other ensure that limit setting works and that kids learn to be accountable and, thus, become responsible individuals.

Here are two conversations that can occur when kids think that they don't have to be accountable:

> Brett is having an "in-depth" talk with his friend on the subject of parental expectations: "You have to sweep the porch? Too bad for you. I don't have to do any of that stuff. My folks never ask me to do anything like that."

> Janine is having a conversation with her friend on the subject of consequences: "You're grounded? For not being home on time!? I never get grounded or anything like that. My parents tell me to do stuff but they never punish me if I don't do it. Lots of times I don't do it. I'm glad I don't live at your house."

Kids know the score. They figure things out pretty quickly. If there are few rules and chores, there is little for them to be accountable for. And in order to ensure cooperation, be sure you have consequences in place (see Chapter Four).

Finally, in two-parent families, both parents must have the same expectations and consequences. Otherwise, the kids will escape being accountable by setting you against one another.

FOUR GUIDELINES FOR LIMIT SETTING

Here are four guidelines for limit setting:

1. *Be clear.* This means be specific. Spell out exactly what you expect: what time to be home, when the room must be cleaned, and how you want it cleaned. Rather than saying, "Be home before dinner," say, "Be home at 5:45." Rather than saying, "Clean your room today," say, "Your room must be cleaned on Saturday before lunch. This means everything must be picked up off the floor, your desk and dresser dusted, and the rug vacuumed."

   This specificity avoids vagueness that can be genuinely misunderstood, or used to a child's advantage: "Gee, I thought dinner was at 6:30." Likewise you must avoid a situation in which, for example, your ten-year-old starts cleaning his room at nine o'clock at night: "You told me to do it today!"

2. *Explain your rules.* Another aspect of being clear is giving explanations to your kids. Child development experts tell us that explanations are very helpful in eliciting cooperation. Kids become involved in the process. Take the time to explain your requirements. Help them understand the reasons for a rule or for a chore. To an older child you might say, "The reason you must be home by 5:45 is that your Dad gets home about that time, and he likes to eat soon after that." To a younger child you might say, "I don't want you going around the corner because then I can't see you. I want to be sure you're okay."

   You don't have to justify to your children what you are doing, but you should let them in on your thinking and allow them to give their reactions. Perhaps they can even help you develop a plan to deal with a certain situation.

3. *Mean what you say and follow through.* Don't give instructions or make rules that you don't care much about. If you really don't care whether the lawn is mowed on a particular day, don't ask that it be done. If you give a consequence, be sure that you intend to enforce it. Don't say, "You can go out to play when you finish doing your homework," and then when a playmate comes over, allow your child to go out to play, without bothering to check whether the homework has been completed.

I know it's easy to be busy with other matters and not pay attention to what is happening at a given moment, but it is important to check whether your direction has been carried out. Following through is part of letting your child know you mean what you say.

4. *Back it up.* This means that you must have consequences for rules and chores. Otherwise, you are dealing with an empty deck. This does not mean you should threaten your children or adopt a punitive attitude. You simply let them know the whole picture. "When you leave your toys out in the yard overnight, they will be put away for a day." "You must eat all of your dinner in order to have dessert." The judicious use of consequences makes your words powerful. (Once again, there is more on this in the next chapter.)

Negotiables and Non-negotiables

When setting rules and responsibilities, decide what is negotiable and what isn't. The specific time to do homework may be negotiable, for example, but bedtime may not be. Being clear about negotiable and non-negotiable matters removes indecisiveness on your part. It makes the boundaries clearer and allows your children to speak up about things that are important to them. They learn to accept the limits you place on them more easily when they know that you will listen to their side and their opinions.

Even though setting limits is extremely important, this does not mean you have to become an autocratic parent. The following sections discuss ways of communicating your expectations to your children that allow them to feel listened to and important.

COMMUNICATING

Communication is a hot topic these days, whether in a large corporation or in an intimate relationship. Communicating is an ongoing, active, and alive process. You cannot overestimate the importance of communication in the family.

Family Meetings

Family meetings promote communicating, are a terrific way to deal with many aspects of family life, and can produce a real sense of togetherness. You can plan activities and vacations, create and adjust schedules, discuss problems, ask for support, set up agreements, make rules, and assign chores, and the list goes on and on. If you have an interesting agenda, it is hard not to communicate with each other. Meetings should be scheduled on a regular basis: once a week or twice a month seems to work best.

One of the major benefits of family meetings is that they allow children to be heard and to have a voice in the running of the family. Everyone, down to the youngest, gets the opportunity to express opinions and have input into family life. When kids can readily see that their parents give serious consideration to what they say, it gives a tremendous boost to family morale. It fosters closeness and caring in the family. This should not be interpreted as meaning that parents give up their authority and let their kids make the rules, but it is important to know how the kids feel about things and to give them a forum in which to express themselves.

Alice and Dwayne were having minor difficulties with all three of their kids. All of them resisted doing their chores and seemed resentful at times. Alice and Dwayne began having family meetings and encouraged the kids to talk about anything they wanted to, especially their feelings and their needs. At first the meetings were dull and rather businesslike. Alice and Dwayne would try to talk about how they could all work together and cooperate with each other, but they got little response.

During the fourth meeting, though, a breakthrough occurred. Mustering his courage, Garrett, age 9, spoke up and said that he thought they all had too much to do. He did not think it was fair that he had to do his chores and his homework right after school every day. Some days he had no time to play with his friends. The younger children agreed with Garrett. Alice and Dwayne listened carefully and told the children that they would think about what they were telling them.

The parents later talked it over and decided that the kids had a valid point. They realized that their expectations had been too high and the kids were feeling cramped. They had created a room that was too small for their kids to operate in.

In the next meeting, the family discussed how they could change the routine so that the kids did not have to do all their chores and homework before they went out to play. They set up a new schedule. Immediately, they saw a change in the kids' attitudes. The resentment almost magically disappeared. Soon they were getting more cooperation. The change was not just due to the rules being more fair. The children also felt that their parents had listened to them. Perhaps the most important value of family meetings is that they are a vehicle for kids to have input into the family in order to feel validated and important.

Feelings

Feelings are a crucial part of communication. Life is not cut-and-dry. We feel all the time, and children have feelings like everyone else, although they may not know how to express them. They may be mad when given a consequence, jealous when a friend gets to do something they can't, hurt when we don't understand them, and scared when they have to face the principal for something they have done wrong. As a parent, you need to pay attention to and relate to your children's feelings. This lets children know you are attuned to them and that their feelings are important to you, which in turn tells them that *they* are important to you. (See the next suggestion box for dealing with feelings.)

How to Deal with Feelings

1. Pay as much attention to how your children are feeling as you do to their behavior.

2. Inquire about their feelings:
   "What are you feeling right now?"
   "You seem sad. Is something wrong?"
   "I noticed that you were mad when you came in for dinner. Do you want to talk about it?"

3. Listen to your child's response. Do not evaluate it or correct it.

4. Acknowledge their feelings:
   "I'm sorry that you had a bad day with Tony."
   "I know you're disappointed that you can't go to the mall with Erika and her mother, but I can't change your dentist appointment."
   "It must feel really awful to be left out of the game."

Sometimes a situation arises in which you can see that your child is clearly at fault. For example, Sean came home from school with a note from his teacher stating that he had started a fight at school. It's easy to start off by giving a lecture or by making a judgmental statement such as "Sean, are you going to grow up to be a bully?" Or "Why do you have to be so mean?" The use of evaluative statements and labels, like *mean* and *bully* can make kids feel unworthy or inadequate. *It is the behavior that is wrong, not the child.* You don't want the child to lose self-respect or self-esteem and identify himself as "I-am-someone-who-does-wrong-and-mean-things." Certainly the child needs to address the wrong he has done. But first deal with him as a person. Inquire about his feelings.

You can ask a general question to allow him to tell you his story: "Sean, tell me what happened." Or, "You must have been pretty mad to start a fight." Once the child knows you will listen to his side, he will feel better and will be more amenable to hearing your side. Listening to his side does not mean you agree with him or that there is no consequence for his behavior. But no matter what your child has done, you want him to know that you believe in him as a person. This will enable him to learn from this experience and ensure that it does not cause a conflict between the two of you.

When setting limits, therefore, pay attention to your child's feelings. Remember that while the behavior may be wrong, feelings are not. When you acknowledge how your children feel, you build an emotional bridge to them and strengthen the bond in your relationship. It is difficult to feel angry at and to resist someone who cares about how you feel. We have all experienced this.

GIVE KIDS CHOICES

Giving children choices empowers them. Making their own decisions helps kids to develop a sense of being in charge of themselves. It increases self-confidence and gives them a sense of mastery in their lives.

This does not mean you give up your power. You simply share it in various ways. To a four-year-old you might say, "Do you want to take a bath before or after dinner?" Taking a bath is not a choice. But the time she takes it is. Giving her this choice involves her in the decision making and gives her a small feeling of power over her life. These small feelings eventually add up to a larger sense of power and a feeling of self-confidence.

To a ten-year-old you might ask, "When do you want to clean your room each week, Friday after school or Saturday morning?" She is capable of deciding which of those alternatives will work best in her life.

But what if she says neither? In that case, listen to her to see if she has a reasonable alternative that works for her and for you. If so, let her decide. It helps her to learn the art of negotiating for what she wants.

But what if the "neither" is really a ploy? What if she just doesn't want to clean her room at all? Then give her another choice: "You can decide when to clean your room, or I will decide for you. Which do you choose?" In this instance, she is deciding how much power she wants, and almost always, children will want to make that decision.

You can also let children choose whether they want a consequence. If there is a problem with misbehavior, such as going outside a prescribed area of play, you might say, "You can play (within this area) and have fun with your friends, or you can play at home without them." This makes it very clear where the responsibility for this behavior lies. And it diminishes arguments when limits are not adhered to, because you only have to refer back to the choice that your child made: "I am sorry you decided to go around the corner without asking me. I am sure you will remember next time. But for the rest of today you must play at home by yourself."

Give your children as many choices as possible. It will empower *them* and make *your* life easier.

SUMMARY

One of the reasons children become uncooperative is that they are not given sufficient responsibilities. Be clear about your expectations, and establish rules and responsibilities that are age appropriate.

Encourage your children to communicate with you, and give them plenty of opportunity to participate in the family decisions. Teach them to negotiate and pay attention to their feelings. Finally, empower them by giving them as many choices as possible.

CHAPTER FOUR

Tools to Keep Limits and Boundaries in Place

*O*nce parents have established clear rules and responsibilities for their children, the next challenge is to get them to comply. This chapter examines several ways of eliciting cooperation in kids. These basic tools can be used in a wide variety of situations.

You might be thinking, "Motivating kids isn't so hard. You simply punish children when they don't do what they're supposed to. You withhold a privilege, or take something they like away from them, or ground them."

Most of us discipline our children by saying: "You can't have dessert." "No TV for you tonight." "You can't go to Amy's." Or, "You have just lost your allowance for this week. Don't be late again." We punish them in the hopes that it will influence their behavior, make them conform to what we want, and deter them from repeating behavior we don't like. Consequences are a powerful way to train kids, although punishment is only one of several kinds of consequences, and not necessarily the best one to use. Let's look at consequences in depth in order to understand how to motivate kids to behave.

CONSEQUENCES

A consequence affects the behavior that precedes it. A positive consequence following a given behavior makes it more likely that the behavior will occur again; a negative consequence makes it less likely that the behavior will occur again. A child finishes a chore and gets to go outside to play. This is a positive result to the behavior. On the other hand, if the child does not finish the chore, he or she does not get to go outside to play. This is a negative consequence. Consequences, therefore, are very powerful in influencing a child's behavior.

Although this is all quite simple and straightforward, it can get more complicated. There is the situation in which the child does not complete the chore but goes outside to play. Now a misbehavior results in a positive consequence. This is not an unusual occurrence and is one of the reasons that children continually misbehave.

Suppose that the child does complete the chore, but then is unexpectedly told to do another chore. Now cooperative behavior results in a negative consequence, at least in the child's mind. And this is important to understand, because consequences vary from child to child and depend on the individual child's likes and dislikes. A positive consequence for one child may not be a positive consequence for another. The same is true for negative consequences.

You need to pay careful attention to the consequences that follow your child's behavior. Here are the possibilities:

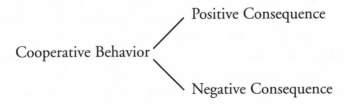

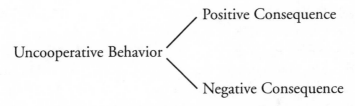

Often parents have difficulties because the consequences following their child's behavior are the direct opposite of what they should be, but they simply don't realize it.

When you set up rules and responsibilities for your kids, you want to set them up this way:

Cooperative Behavior ➤ Positive Consequence

Uncooperative Behavior ➤ Negative Consequence

Once examined, this may seem perfectly obvious; however, in day-to-day living, it is not always easy to recognize and put into practice. Let's look at a more complicated example: Janet consulted me about her third grade daughter, Rachel, who was doing poorly in school. While Rachel complained that school was too hard, the main reason for her poor performance was that she was not studying, was doing her homework irregularly, and occasionally missed the school bus. Sometimes she would forget to bring her books home, and sometimes she would forget to take them to school. Rachel was quite forgetful, it turned out; in fact, she was something of a medical mystery—senility at the age of eight.

As Janet and I looked into this situation, we discovered that Janet tried very hard to help Rachel. In fact, she tried too hard. When Rachel forgot her books, Janet would make a special trip to bring her books to school or to retrieve them. When Rachel missed the school bus, Janet would drive her. When Rachel had a report to do, she would wait until the last night to do it, and Janet would spend the evening helping her, sometimes practically doing the report for her.

Rachel seldom had any negative consequences for her forgetting, lateness, and procrastination. Actually, she had positive consequences for her behavior. Janet drove her to school and did her homework for her. In a larger sense, Rachel didn't have to take responsibility for her behavior. Janet rescued her, and in so doing made her life too easy. As a result, Rachel was not developing the self-discipline needed to grow and mature into a responsible person. Janet did not realize that she was providing positive consequences for undesirable behavior.

Once Janet realized this, however, she made changes. She explained to Rachel what the problem was and how things were going to change. When she missed the bus, she would have to walk. (They lived fairly close to the school.) When she forgot to bring her books home, she would not be allowed to use the phone for the evening or to watch TV.

Of course, Rachel was not at all pleased and put up some resistance initially. But once she realized that Janet meant business, she slowly adapted to the new situation. She was late for school a few times because she missed the bus and had to walk, but when she received detention as a result, she began being on time for the school bus. Since Janet was no longer doing her work for her, she had to deal with teachers who were not pleased with her performance. Eventually she understood what was expected of her, and gradually she stopped "forgetting." She became more responsible.

One of the first things to look for when your child is not complying is whether the misbehavior has positive consequences. Let's look at various kinds of consequences that are effective in motivating children to cooperate.

Natural Consequences

Natural consequences come about naturally following a particular behavior. If you don't bother to put gas in your car, you'll soon be inconvenienced when your car comes to a stop in the middle of the street or, even worse, on the freeway.

The consequence of being late or being inconvenienced will be a strong reminder in the future to check your gas tank.

Letting children experience the natural consequences for misbehavior whenever possible is one of the most effective ways to train them. For example, if a child procrastinates and is late getting to a friend's house for a ride to the swimming pool, she misses her ride and can't go swimming. If a child forgets his money for the movie, he can't get in.

With natural consequences, you let life teach your child the lessons he or she needs to learn. *There is no need for you to add any further sanctions.* Let your child deal with the problem. Don't take the child to the pool, and don't make a special trip to the movie theater to give him the money. Let your children learn to be responsible through the lessons that naturally come about. (Of course, following the principle of natural consequences is not about being hard hearted. If on a rare occasion your child is late or forgets something, of course you help him or her out.)

Problem Situation: What do you do if your child leaves his bike out on the front lawn overnight and in the morning it is gone? Do you punish him for being careless? Do you rush down to the bicycle shop and buy him a new one? Do you punish him first and then buy him a new bike?

Ask yourself what the problem is and what the natural consequence is. The problem is that he has been careless. The consequence is that he no longer has a bike. Whose problem is it that he no longer has a bike? It is his, of course. The loss of the bike is the consequence. It is already in place as a result of his action.

This is not an easy situation to deal with. If it is a brand new bike that you spent big bucks on, or if carelessness on the part of your child has been an ongoing issue, there is a very good chance that you would be upset. It would be tempting to lecture, punish, and generally carry on about it. On the other side, it is a situation made to order for a parent with a "pleasing" style, a parent who doesn't want his or her child to suffer and who would be sorely tempted after a short while to buy a new bike.

It is certainly natural enough on your part to feel some or all of these things. But neither buying a new bike nor fussing and fuming will help the situation. In fact, both reactions will get in the way of your child learning a lesson. There will either be no consequences for his behavior or he will likely get caught up in your upset and react to your reaction, which can distract him from the lesson at hand.

The most effective response is simply to let your child deal with the consequences of losing his bike. Let him deal with not having fun riding with his friends or being unable to go certain places because it is too far to walk. It will be hard seeing your child lose out. After a while, it will be tempting to step in and buy him a new bike, especially if his birthday is coming soon. But this would reward him for his carelessness. Talk about a positive consequence for undesirable behavior!

Employ Natural Consequences

1. Do not criticize, rescue, or impose additional punishments:
   Criticism: "How could you lose your allowance? Don't you know how to take care of things?"
   Rescuing: "Oh, it's okay. Here's some money."
   Punishment: "You're losing next week's allowance as well. You need to learn your lesson."

2. Deal with the problem only:
   "I'm sorry you lost your allowance. I hope you take better care of it next week."
   "You'll have to wait until next week to buy that baseball."

   These suggestions are powerful, because the child has only himself or herself to deal with, and not the emotional reactions of parents.

Then what do you do? Talk to him about it. Help him to think it through so that he can learn from the situation. Perhaps after a few days, you can help him work out a plan to get another bike. If he is old enough, he can mow lawns in the neighborhood. Or you could hire him to do jobs around the house. Pay him what you would pay anyone else, and don't make it real easy. Earning the money for a new bike needs to be a slow process. Every week he can see how much money is going into his bicycle kitty. Don't pressure him to do the jobs to make the money. It is up to him. If he doesn't want to make the effort to obtain a new bike, that is his choice. Let him live with it.

Eventually, if you see that your child is no longer careless and that he has done a consistent job of earning money, you might say, "I think you have learned your lesson. Now you know how to be careful, and you have really worked hard to get a new bike. You have saved almost enough to buy a new one. I am going to help you. I will pay the last $20 you need. Let's go down to the bike shop today." Thus, you reward industriousness and perseverance, and, in addition, you show your child that you care about him.

Logical Consequences

Natural consequences cannot handle every situation. Some situations are dangerous, such as a young child playing in the street, and many situations really have no natural consequence, such as not doing the dishes or not picking up the toys in the living room. These situations require the parent to intervene and create consequences. These are called Logical Consequences.

Tie logical consequences as closely as possible to the behavior in question. Suppose that your five-year-old disobeys the rule that she must play in front of the house. You find that she has gone around the corner to her friend's. Rather than spanking her or telling her that she cannot watch TV that night, the logical consequence could be that she has to stay in the house or in the backyard for some specified period of time. If you have a problem with your seven-year-old not putting his toys away, you can set up a consequence in which the toys that are not put away at bedtime are put on a shelf in the closet for a few days.

Logical consequences that relate to activities and privileges are usually the most effective. You have to tailor them to your particular child. They could include, for example, extra playtime, the use of the phone, a sleepover at a friend's, or being allowed to stay up later than usual to watch a special program on TV.

Be sure that you are fair and reasonable. This is not about being punitive. Punitiveness can result when you feel you must punish your children to teach them a lesson. *You* do not have to teach them a lesson or do a lot of talking. Let the consequence teach them the lesson. Anything else will just get in the way. When the little rascals challenge you, simply remind them of the rule and consequence. There is no need for lengthy discussions or arguments. And remember to be firm and gentle.

The Famous Saturday-Morning-Soccer-Game

Letting children take the consequences, natural or logical, for their behavior is one of the hardest things for parents to do. Let's look at the famous Saturday-morning-soccer-game, also known in some circles as a visit to the Heartbreak Hotel.

Although Kevin, age seven, was one of the better players on his soccer team, he was not as good at doing his chores as he was at playing soccer. Often his team had games on Saturday mornings, and this coincided with his responsibility to clean his room. He usually had an eleven o'clock game. When the time came to leave for the game on the first Saturday of the season, however, Kevin's room had not been cleaned. Kevin's parents decided to let him go to the game. After all, one of the best players should not be late or miss the game. They told him that he could clean his room after the game.

That afternoon the room was not cleaned. Kevin was "too tired" after the game. Several skirmishes between Kevin and his parents ensued, and all in all, it was not a pleasant afternoon.

The next week his parents were determined that his room would be cleaned before the game. They got him up a half-hour early, and throughout the morning they frequently checked on him and reminded him to get the room done. Actually, they fell into the nagging style described in Chapter One. They did not want him to be late for the game and did not want to let the team down. When time came to leave for the game, the room was not cleaned. They took him to the game, and another unpleasant Saturday afternoon ensued.

Finally, his parents realized they had to be much firmer. After all, what was more important in the long run, playing soccer or learning to be responsible? They decided to set up some consequences to his behavior. The next week, they told Kevin that the rule to clean his room on Saturday mornings was still in effect. Once he finished cleaning his room, he could do whatever he wanted, including playing soccer. This was the logical consequence.

Naturally, Kevin did not take his parents seriously. When his room was not cleaned in time to leave for the game on the next Saturday, his parents refused to take him. At first, Kevin was dumbfounded. This was followed by a period of ranting. However, his parents did not waver. Without arguing with him, they simply told him that it was up to him whether he played soccer. When Kevin finally calmed down, he realized that he was dealing with a new breed of parents—parents who meant what they said. He dove into cleaning his room. When he finished, his parents took him to the game, which was almost over. The coach did not put him in the game. His parents explained to the coach what had happened, and the coach understood and did not penalize Kevin any further.

Yes, ladies and gentlemen, this is a sad story. It was heart breaking that Kevin missed most of his game and did not get to play. But after this incident, he knew that if he wanted to play soccer, he had to do his chore. Guess who cleaned his room on Saturday mornings and never missed a game after that? The logical consequences worked.

The consequences were both positive or negative. If Kevin didn't clean his room, he didn't play soccer. If he did, then he could play. Kevin's parents allowed him to choose. Moreover, they remained dispassionate. They did not get upset or carry on. As much as possible, children need to experience the consequences for their behavior. It is a relatively easy and efficient way to train them.

Punishment

I am going to say it right up front: **Don't use punishment.** You are probably thinking, "Wait just a minute, Mr. Psychologist. You've just been advocating natural and logical consequences. Aren't they the same thing as punishment?" They are similar in that both are negative consequences, but there are some differences between them that make one far more effective than the other. Punishment and logical consequences differ in the state of mind of the parent and the effect on the child. Let's define punishment.

The dictionary defines *punish* as (1) to cause to undergo pain and (2) to inflict a penalty for an offense. The basic idea, then, when punishing children is that if they suffer some pain and incur a penalty they won't misbehave. Punishment acts as a deterrent for undesirable behavior.

When you use punishment, therefore, you have to cause your child some pain. It creates a state of mind: "Let's make 'em hurt so they don't do it again." I don't know about you, but this does not seem like a particularly appealing approach to me. Actually, it is the same idea that is used to deal with criminals.

It is not necessary for you to inflict pain to change uncooperative behavior, although there may well be pain involved. If you use natural and logical consequences, then the events in your child's life or the consequences from broken agreements will cause the discomfort and pain for her. But you are no longer in the role of punisher, the inflictor of pain. This can make a big difference in your relationship with your children.

You want to be as dispassionate as possible when disciplining your child. When parents "lose their cool," they are more likely to give inappropriate punishment, to be harsh, and to be inconsistent, and they are more likely to fall into one of these modes when in the role of punisher.

Recently I heard that one parent, when confronted with a difficult situation, grounded her child for a year. What did this child, a nine-year-old, do to deserve such a punishment? She must have robbed a bank or burned down her school. Well, of course, she did nothing like this. But she did do something serious. She had not done her homework for three weeks and, when questioned about it, lied to her parents. There is no question that this is a serious problem. But will grounding her for a year teach her the lesson she needs to learn? It absolutely will not. It will only make her very resentful. Will doing something more reasonable, such as grounding her for a week, teach her the lesson she needs to learn? It's not likely that this will do it either.

This parent was desperate and angry, and didn't know what to do, although she undoubtedly felt pressure to do something. Because she acted out of these feelings, the punishment was inappropriate and harsh. Of course, we all get angry sometimes, but being the punisher will not solve the problem. Such a reaction will create heavy resentment in the child and negatively impact the parent-child relationship.

Using punishment as the main or only means of correcting misbehavior can set up problems in the parent-child relationship. When a parent says, "I am going to punish you," children hear this statement in different ways. They may hear it as "I am going to get even with you." They may hear it as "I have more power than you." They may even hear it as "I want to hurt you."

These reactions in children create emotional side effects and problems in the relationship, even though the parents have no intentions of hurting their children or getting even. But when punishment is used over and over again, kids react to what they think the intention is. This can set up a negative undertone in the relationship, create resentment, and actually increase the child's resistance.

Kids may say, "You're not being fair." Or they may say "You're mean." Such expressions indicate that they are relating to you as the punisher. However, with natural and logical consequences, this is much less likely to happen because you are not in the role of punisher. You are dispassionate and simply allow the consequences to come into play. The consequence approach is more effective, even when the consequence and the punishment are the same thing.

There is no reason to use physical punishment. Such punishment induces fear in kids, and fear is a negative motivator. Rather than moving toward something positive, they must try to avoid something they fear. Physical punishment leads parents into authoritarian roles, and authoritarian parents risk quashing their kids' resourcefulness and creativity.

In addition, physical punishment sometimes creates incongruent situations. If a parent hits her child for hitting a playmate, for example, what lesson will the child learn?

Punishment and natural and logical consequences, then, have different effects on kids. Punishment can make kids feel fearful and resentful. These feelings negatively impact the parent-child relationship and can have a long-term impact. Using natural and logical consequences, on the other hand, is a more objective and dispassionate way of disciplining children, and as a result there are far fewer negative emotional side effects on the parent-child relationship. Kids are more likely to take responsibility for the result of their actions when consequences are employed rather than when punishment is doled out. Therefore, consequences are far more effective.

Dealing with the Unexpected

Although I have been stressing that you need to have clear rules and responsibilities laid out for your kids, you can't anticipate every situation and problem that could arise, and often you have to handle things on the spot. For example, you walk into the kitchen to find that your five-year-old has eaten some cookies that were left out and has ruined her appetite for dinner. Or, you discover that your ten-year-old has taken a ride across town with the teenager next door, without your permission. How do you handle these situations?

In most cases, the best procedure is to set the new rule and specify the consequence, but not to apply it on this first occasion. It is best not to create logical consequences for things that are not clear or have not been agreed upon in advance. Let the first time act as a warning.

Tell your five-year old: "You have eaten cookies without asking me and now you will not be hungry when dinner-time comes. You cannot have cookies or any food unless you ask first. The next time that you eat cookies without asking me, you will not be allowed to have cookies or any sweets for _____ (specify the time period)."

This statement explains the problem clearly and gives the consequence. At the same time it allows some leeway, since that particular situation had not been addressed until now. Don't be punitive; simply state the new rule and the consequence.

Tell your ten-year-old: "It is not okay to go anywhere out of the neighborhood without asking me first, and certainly not to take a ride with anyone without asking me. I am surprised you did this, and I hope this rule is now clear to you. This is a very serious matter. If it should happen again, you will be not be allowed to go anywhere for _____ (specify the time period)."

In this situation you may feel that your child should have known better, that at age ten she should have figured out that she was to ask you first. And you are probably right. But it won't help to say something like: "You should have known better than to do something like this." She already knows she should have known better. Just set the limit without in any way "making her wrong." You might say: "I hope this is perfectly clear to you, and I know you will use good judgment from now on."

Furthermore, you do not have to figure everything out the moment it happens. You may need some time to think the situation over. You can talk it over with your spouse and then lay out the new rule and the consequence. And don't forget: If you realize anywhere along the way that your child's style is oppositional, then stop everything and deal with that first.

REWARDS—POSITIVE MOTIVATORS

For some time Larry's parents had been encountering stiff resistance from him about doing his chores. Hearing about rewards as a way to motivate kids, they decided to try this approach. The fact that it was a positive way to discipline appealed to them.

One of ten-year-old Larry's chores consisted of emptying all of the wastebaskets in the house each week and putting out the garbage cans. They told him that they would give him $1 each week to do these chores. The next week the trash was emptied and the garbage put out. The following week the same routine. Larry's parents felt good. They had finally found a way to get him to cooperate.

A couple of weeks later Larry approached his parents with a deal: If they would pay him only $15 a month, he'd go to school—no money down, just easy weekly payments. "It's only fifty cents a day," the little salesman declared. Larry was also quite good at math.

Of course, I made up the last part of the story. But the question remains. Should you give your children candy or toys or other material rewards for cooperative behavior? In other words, should you pay your kids to be good—to do what they're supposed to do anyway?

Before we answer this question, let's consider a few things. First, what exactly is a reward? A reward is a positive consequence to a behavior that makes it more likely the behavior will occur again. If you walked down Main Street and someone handed you a hundred-dollar bill, chances are that you would come back soon to see if the same thing could happen again. If it did, you would probably spend a lot of time on Main Street. The hundred-dollar reward would influence your behavior, and you would probably come back every day or every hour as long as that person continued to hand out hundred-dollar bills.

Becoming aware of rewards is important because they influence behavior powerfully in the family environment, whether you are aware of them or not. I like to divide rewards into three categories: Interpersonal rewards, material rewards, and privileges.

Interpersonal rewards include our attention, recognition, approval, and affection—our natural ways of being and interacting with our kids. These rewards shape and influence their behavior. I call them "interpersonal rewards" because they are just that. They occur naturally and spontaneously in our interactions with our children. And they occur all the time. So we need to be aware of what behaviors we are influencing.

As you have undoubtedly noticed, families are quite different from each other. Some parents value a quiet, orderly lifestyle and support and approve of behaviors in their children that conform to that way of living. It is not necessarily something they consciously think about. Other parents value more boisterous behavior and encourage and reward with their attention such activities as joking and telling stories. They may even compete with each other to see who can tell the funniest story. The kids in these two types of families will act and behave differently.

You also need to remember that natural ways of interacting can also reward behaviors that you do not value or find undesirable. Often parents unwittingly reward oppositional styles and misbehavior, for example, by listening to an arguing child. Be careful not to reward unwanted behaviors with your time and attention.

Acknowledge with your attention and approval only appropriate behaviors. Tell your kids, for example, that you appreciate them doing the dishes right after supper or coming home on time. Let them know that it makes life easier for you, and give them a hug. Like anyone else, kids like to be acknowledged and appreciated. It makes them feel good. This positive approach powerfully promotes the behavior you want.

Material rewards for children include money, candy, and toys. When you want to influence a particular behavior, you can introduce material rewards systematically, as in the example with Larry cited previously. However, even though such rewards work, at least for a while, it is not a good idea to pay kids to do what you want. Using money, toys, and sweets as incentives to elicit cooperation creates other problems. It is hard in practice to wean children from them, and it sets up a strange dynamic in which, rather than developing a more fundamental sense of responsibility, they expect to be paid for contributing to family life. (In the same vein, allowances should not be tied to work around the house.) I do not recommend the use of material rewards as the main way to train children. However, very occasionally you might give a material reward as a special acknowledgment.

Privileges offer a very powerful means to influence children's behavior. One way to do this is to tie privileges to responsibilities.

"When you finish loading the dishwasher, you can watch TV."
"After you clear the front lawn of your toys and bikes, you can play with your friends."
"Since you have gone to bed on time all week, you can stay up an extra hour tonight."

These privileges serve as rewards for following rules and handling responsibilities. They are positive consequences for desired behavior. And the atmosphere is positive. Training kids and teaching them to be responsible does not have to be filled with pain and suffering.

Use interpersonal rewards and privileges as the main ways to influence your child's behavior. On occasion, you might use a material reward in the following way: "Since you've done such a good job sweeping the kitchen and taking out the garbage, I think I can spare a dollar to help you buy that spaceman you've been wanting."

Acknowledge and Promote Small Changes

When you are trying to change a misbehavior, acknowledge any positive change, even if it is not yet exactly what you want. For instance, if you are trying to change whining and you notice that the whining is less shrill or does not last as long as usual, let your child know you can see that they are making an effort. "You did not whine as much this time. That's much better. I can see you are trying." Or, if it is a problem with picking up items that have been left on the floor, you can say, "You picked up some of your clothes off the floor this time. I appreciate it. Keep trying. I know you can pick them all up."

This is far better than saying, "You're still whining. When are you going to stop?" Or, sternly, "There are still clothes on the floor." *Acknowledge and encourage.* It works wonders.

Behavior usually does not change all at once. It changes bit by bit. Therefore, acknowledge the "bits." Your child will feel good, and so will you. It will point your child in the direction you want, painlessly.

Of course, you will have to impose consequences for misbehavior from time to time. However, if you use rewards to promote and encourage the behavior you want, there will be less resistance, fewer misbehaviors, fewer negative consequences, and much more fun around the ranchero.

MODELING

No, I am not about to discuss getting your children into a line of work. Modeling is a way for parents to direct their children.

Modeling goes beyond simply telling your children what you want; it shows them exactly how to do things and how you want them to behave, including how they talk to you. You become the model and put on a demonstration for them. For example, show your kids how you want them to clean their rooms and how you want the dishwasher stacked. Do it with them the first time. Or show them how to talk to you; say the words for them. Show them what constitutes an effective style of relating by giving them very specific and clear instructions. (Modeling is discussed further in Chapter Five.)

It is worth taking the time to model for your children because kids learn especially well by watching and imitating. (We all do.) Also, when you are having problems, you can say, "Remember how I showed you to do this? That is how I want it done." Teaching your children by modeling for them makes things quite clear. It is a powerful teaching tool.

Of course, we are models not only at those times when *we* decide to instruct them. Because they constantly watch what we say and do, we are modeling for them all the time. The implications are clear.

SUMMARY

Here are the major tools you now have to generate obedience and cooperation in your children and that will enable limit setting to work:

> *Natural Consequences:* These consequences follow a given behavior and are naturally corrective. Let them come into play whenever possible. There is no need to add any further consequences.
>
> *Logical Consequences:* These consequences must be set up by you. Try to set them up in advance and to relate them to the behavior as much as possible. This helps you to be

calm and dispassionate, even in trying situations, making discipline more effective.

Rewards: The best rewards are interpersonal—your attention, approval, and affection. Use these to foster the behavior you want. You can also use privileges as rewards; they are especially useful for keeping agreements and handling responsibilities.

Modeling: Show your children the behavior you want. Modeling is especially helpful when dealing with oppositional styles. Using modeling and rewards together is a powerful way to train new behavior. Acknowledge the "bits," or any small changes in the desired direction. Think of changing misbehavior as a series of small steps.

REVIEW

You now have all the tools you need to discipline your children. Here is a review of the main points that have been explained in the book thus far:

1. The most important way to teach kids to comply and cooperate is to teach them to be respectful of others. This starts at home by training them to interact and relate appropriately and acceptably. Therefore, you must pay close attention to how your kids talk to you in ordinary, day-to-day situations and not allow negative styles to develop; or, if they have developed, correct them, using the tools you have learned in the last two chapters.

2. If you have a child who is misbehaving, first address his or her oppositional ways of relating and reacting. The way your child relates to you is the key to obtaining compliance. (When you teach a difficult-to-manage child to relate respectfully, at least seventy-five percent of your problem will be handled.)

3. Set limits and boundaries by giving your children rules and responsibilities.
4. To keep the boundaries intact, use natural and logical consequences, rewards (interpersonal rewards and privileges), and modeling as your main tools.

The next section discusses how to handle specific problems and persistent misbehavior. One word of caution: Some difficulties with children are due to unresolved emotional problems. If you try these techniques and do not get the results you want, you may need to seek professional guidance.

The Ten Most Prevalent Discipline Situations and How to Handle Them

*I*n Part Three, all of the principles and strategies that have been discussed are applied to a wide variety of problems and situations that arise when disciplining children. The misbehaviors in each chapter have similar causes and/or similar solutions.

Chapters Five and Six are especially important because they deal with children's styles of relating, which, as has been stressed throughout the book, are the most important aspect of discipline. When children talk and relate respectfully, parents find that setting limits and correcting them is far easier than when children have resistive styles. (In the remaining chapters, it is assumed that *oppositional styles are addressed first, before dealing with the misbehavior.*)

Chapters Seven through Thirteen deal with common, yet challenging, issues that arise in day-to-day living. Since you can't avoid or escape them, it is best to know how to handle them.

Chapter Fourteen is concerned with disciplining the child who is difficult to handle, who exhibits multiple misbehaviors. It shows you how to correct the child who can't be corrected.

Finally, Chapter Fifteen offers some questions and answers in areas that parents have frequently asked me about over the years.

The premise in this book, and particularly in Part Three, is that you can be in charge of your children, and if problems arise, you can fix them. You may be confused or have lost your way a bit; but believe me, you have not lost your power. You just need to know where it is.

Now, let's find it!

CHAPTER FIVE

Whining and Arguing: "Why Can't I? Why Can't I? Why Can't I?"

*F*our-year-old Ally is unhappy that Mom said she could not have a cookie: "I want a cookie (squeak). I waaaant (squeak) a cookie. (squeak). Why (squeak) can't I have (squeak) a cookie?" This is the not-so-sweet sound of one child whining.

Ten-year-old Andy is arguing with his father: "Why can't I go over to Jeff's? It's just for an hour. You let Billy go to his friend's. You never let me do anything, Dad." Andy repeats his position several times, each time more vigorously.

It's only natural that kids will respond in resistive ways from time to time. They will whine, complain, cry, argue, demand, and so forth when they don't get their way. These are level-one and level-two styles of responding. Although you must expect this from time to time, you don't want these responses to become your child's regular and automatic way of relating to you. This chapter shows how to handle whining, arguing, and any level-one or level-two oppositional style. And it looks at how to prevent these responses from becoming problematic styles to begin with.

As a reminder, here are typical responses at each level:

Level one: whining, complaining, nagging
Level two: arguing, pleading, talking back, bossing

HOW OPPOSITIONAL WAYS OF RELATING DEVELOP

The main reason that children develop undesirable styles is that parents unwittingly reward them for this behavior in their interactions with them. It is impossible to remain unresponsive at all times to a child's negative tone and manner, so I am not suggesting anything heroic. However, if you know how the patterns come about, you will be less likely to allow them to get established in the first place.

Unfortunately, it is remarkably easy to train children to relate in ways that we find undesirable, and most of the time parents are quite unaware of how they do this. It's not that we directly show them how to be negative. We don't sit our children down and say, "Here is how you whine." Or, "Here is how you defy. Go ahead. Give it a try." "No, no, that's not quite right. Do it this way." Of course, this is silly. Or is it? While we may not directly train them, what we do amounts to the same thing. It is just more subtle.

There are two main ways in which resistive and oppositional styles can be rewarded. One way these rewards occur is when a parent gives in to the child. For example, Ally's mother can't stand the whining anymore, so after five or ten minutes of clenching her teeth, she lets Ally have the cookie even though dinner is only an hour away. While this brings Ally's mother temporary relief, it is a step in the wrong direction because giving Ally the cookie rewards her whining behavior; and since Ally is no dummy, she will figure it out: "When I whine, I get what I want." In fact, she may even think: "If I whine long enough, I'll get what I want." Thus, perseverance may also be rewarded. Since Ally got her cookie, she is poised to try the whining approach again. I'll give you odds on that.

Another way to encourage the development of a resistive style is by listening and attending to your child when he or she is talking to you in rude or disrespectful ways. As we saw in the last chapter, your attention is the reward and, therefore, encourages this behavior. Simply by giving your time and attention to whining or arguing, just by listening without any comment, you reward these ways of relating, and the undesired style is likely to recur. Another way of looking at these kinds of situations is that you are implicitly giving your kids permission to speak in negative ways.

Now this can be quite subtle; it can occur even when you are setting a limit. For example, Andy is arguing with his mother about emptying the dishwasher:

> "I don't want to empty the dishwasher. It's Linda's turn."
> "No, it is your turn, Andy."
> "No, it isn't. I did it last night."
> "Andy, it's your turn because you traded with her the night before."
> "Mom, this isn't fair."
> "You have to empty the dishwasher, Andy."
> "Mom, you're never fair."

The problem in this situation is that even though Mom is trying to set a limit, she is engaging Andy while he is arguing with her, allowing him to argue and providing an interpersonal reward. Therefore, he will likely keep arguing with her.

What Mom needs to focus on first is how Andy is talking to her—his style in that moment—so that she can deal with it.

This is not easy to do when you are being pulled into an argument. (See the box below for some suggestions.)

Pay attention to how your children talk to you and don't let a style creep up on you. Again, this does not call for heroics. Just be tuned in to how your children relate and interact.

Prevent Oppositional Styles from Developing

1. Notice how your children talk and interact with you. Awareness is crucial.

2. Do not reward resistive styles with your attention, by granting requests or by giving in.

3. Correct the style. (See the Suggestion Box, Nip Oppositional Styles in the Bud, in Chapter Two.)

HOW TO CHANGE WHINING, ARGUING, AND ANY OTHER LEVEL-ONE OR LEVEL-TWO OPPOSITIONAL STYLES

When a child has a negative style, it means that the style is embedded and automatic. Unless you have the right tools, it is usually quite a challenge to change this style. It will take time, effort, and consistency on your part.

I always recommend to parents that they try the simplest approach first:

1. As stated previously, stop rewarding the style.
2. Reward the style you want.

Suppose your child is whining constantly. Tell him you will not listen to him when he is whining, and, therefore, he cannot have whatever it is that he wants. Then acknowledge him whenever he does not whine when he does not get something he wants or when you have set a limit. Tell him you appreciate it, and give him a big smile and a hug. On occasion you might even throw in a privilege as a bonus: "You may stay up for an extra half-hour tonight, and we'll play a game because you have been talking so nicely."

Another way to stop rewarding a resistive style is to introduce a logical consequence instead. Since one reward for your child is your attention, try this: Tell her that she can whine, but you do not want to listen to it. Then give her a choice: "You may stay in the house and not whine or you may go out in the backyard and whine. Which will it be?" Then follow through. Whining to herself in the backyard will not be much fun.

Because oppositional styles can become so automatic and embedded, these interventions may not always work. The following is an even more powerful way to change negative styles.

Use Modeling along with Rewards to Change Oppositional Styles

Modeling is especially useful when you want to correct a negative style. In fact, combining modeling with natural rewards for the behavior you want is an extraordinarily powerful way to correct oppositional styles. There are four steps in this process:

1. Explain the problem and describe the desired behavior.
2. Model the style you want.
3. Have your child practice it, and acknowledge (reward) positive changes during practice.
4. Deal with the style in real-life situations.

Do not try this procedure when you are under direct fire from an oppositional style. Choose a time when things are relatively quiet so that you will have your child's attention without any interruptions.

Let's return to Ally as an example of how to use this procedure. Suppose that Ally's whining has gone unchecked, and now
she does not whine as much; however, you have a bossy deman-
der on your hands (a level-two style). Her manner is "Give me
this." "I want that." "Take me to the park right now." She has
had a few temper tantrums as well; but after observing her closely, you realize that her bossiness is the style that occurs most frequently. Next, go through the four steps with the little boss:

1. **Explain:** Sit Ally down and explain the problem:
   "Ally, here is how you talk to me. This morning you
   said, 'Give me a cookie.' That is not okay. I don't want
   you to talk to me like that and in that tone of voice. You
   must ask me nicely when you want something."
   Take your time, and be sure that she understands.

2. **Model:** Show Ally how you want her to talk to you:
   "When you want something, I don't want you to tell
   me or to boss me. Here is how I want you to ask me:
   'Dad, may I have a cookie?' Or, if you want to go to
   the park, 'Dad, could you take me to the park today?'
   I want you to ask politely. Do you understand what I
   want you to do?"
   Be sure she understands.

3. **Practice:** The next phase is to let your child try it.
   This is called role playing, a technique for trying out
   new behaviors. Say to your child:

   "Ally, let's pretend. Suppose you want a cookie. How will
   you ask me from now on?"
   "I don't know."
   "Well, remember how I just said it? 'Dad may I have a
   cookie?' Try it."
   "Dad, can I have a cookie?"

"That's terrific, Ally. That's how I want you to ask for things from now on. Suppose you want to go to the playground with your friends. How would you ask me?"

"Dad, will you take me to the playground?"

"That's it. That's how I want you to talk to your mom and me. Will you try to remember it when you want something?"

"Yes."

"I am happy you are going to try this. I think it will be better for us, and we won't get mad at each other so much."

Of course, this procedure may not go as smoothly as this at first. But just stay with it until you are satisfied that your child knows clearly what you want. This is role playing, and you have created a model for your child. Now, what do you do in real-life situations?

4. **Real Life:** The first time Ally wants something, she will probably forget the conversation altogether. There is no need to get upset. Don't forget that styles are ingrained habits. Just gently remind her:

    "Remember what we talked about this morning? About how to ask me for what you want?"

    "Yes."

    "Then try it again. How do you ask me?"

Let her try it again and acknowledge any improvement.

If when you ask her to recall the conversation about asking, she says she doesn't remember, then go over it again with her, even if you are pretty sure she does remember. Keep the approach positive. Then say:

    "Now try it again. Ask me if you can go over to Jodie's."

    (Sigh) "Can I go to Jodie's?"

    "That's better. I appreciate it when you ask me like that."

Ignore the sigh. Her behavior is improved. Acknowledge the "bits"—the improvement, however small—in her style. And be prepared to do this as many times as it takes.

Be sure to distinguish between her style and the request. These are separate issues, and you should deal with them separately. Many times you will reward and acknowledge the change in style and deny the request: "No, you can't go to the park right now, but I appreciate how nicely you asked me."

But if at all possible when you are starting this kind of training, grant the request. It is an extra reward for the child's attempt to make changes. If you can't grant the request, you can say: "We can go tomorrow."

You will have to work with this a number of times until the new style becomes habitual, and you both may struggle with these changes for a while. Once you start, be consistent, and keep at it until the behavior is changed. When you see a clear improvement, throw in the bonus, an extra special reward: "Ally, you've been talking so nicely and not whining, your Dad and I are going to take you to Disney World for a week." Of course, I'm exaggerating, but a Disney movie will do the trick. It is an extra reward and privilege for her hard work.

This approach can work with any style. However, it is important to remember to start with the less intense ones.

CHAPTER SIX

Defiance and Tantrums: "You Can't Make Me! You Can't Make Me! You Can't Make Me"

*C*ory, age five, has been rolling on the floor of the living room, flailing his legs, and screaming for nearly five minutes. His mom is about to pass out.

Gene, age eight, is yelling at his Dad, "I hate you. I'm not cleaning my room, and you can't make me. You're a snothead!" Now his Dad is about to pass out.

These situations portray life with children in the emotional fast lane. The parents have lost control of the children, and the children have lost control of themselves. Unconsciousness doesn't seem like such a bad choice; in fact, next to relaxing on a tropical isle, it seems like quite a wonderful place to be. This chapter develops strategies to deal with these very intense oppositional styles, those at levels three and four. Here is a review of these styles:

Level three: defying, threatening, demanding, yelling, antagonizing, and being belligerent

Level four: screaming, throwing tantrums (including throwing things, slamming doors, and running away while being corrected)

Like whining and arguing, these styles develop because they are rewarded. Sometimes a child discovers that a level-two style, such as arguing, doesn't get what she wants, but when she yells, Dad gives in. She "upped the ante" to a level-three style and found that she got the result she wanted. Once again, be aware and don't reward these styles.

THE GOAL IS SELF-CONTROL

When a child is regularly defiant and belligerent and/or having tantrums of some kind, he is having a problem with self-control. It is certainly all right for children to disagree with their parents and to express their displeasure. However, they need to be able to contain themselves in the process. They learn this containment when their parents set limits on them, thus creating external boundaries for them. As time goes on, they internalize this process and gradually learn to set these boundaries for themselves. This means they are able to regulate their behavior from within.

Another way of stating this issue is that in order for children to control themselves, their parents must first have control over them. When children fall into defiance and tantrums, levels three and four, as ways of interacting, neither they themselves nor their parents have control. It is vital, then, that parents do not allow their kids to operate at levels three and four and that they know how to manage intense oppositional styles.

This leaves a minor question to be answered. Where do you start when you have a child who is yelling or screaming or having tantrums several times a day? Well, one thing we all know from our experience is that it is almost impossible to deal with kids when this behavior is in full swing.

HOW TO CHANGE DEFIANCE, TANTRUMS, OR ANY INTENSE OPPOSITIONAL STYLE

In Chapter Two we saw that when a child has one or more level-three and level-four styles operating, there will invariably be level-one and level-two styles operating at high frequencies. Therefore, don't start by trying to change the defiance or tantrums. *The first step is to change the least intense oppositional or resistive style with which your child engages you.* (See the following Suggestion Box.)

Gene, the Eight-year-old "Defier"

Following a period of observation, Gene's parents discovered that he whined and complained constantly. Rather than continuing to focus on his defiance, they set up a strategy to change his whining and complaining. First, they stopped rewarding the whining with their time and attention and used modeling and rewards (as outlined previously) to elicit and encourage an acceptable way of interacting with them. Of course, they had some setbacks along the way; but after about three weeks, Gene's whining and complaining had gone from an average of five to twelve times a day to hardly occurring at all.

How to Handle Defiance and Tantrums

1. Observe your child to discover the least intense style in his repertoire. This will be a level-one or a level-two style.

2. Select this style to change first.

3. Follow the suggestions given in Chapter Five for changing level-one and level-two styles.

Then, Gene's parents noticed an astonishing and wondrous void. They had been so focused on helping him with his whining and complaining that they had not noticed that his defiance had also significantly diminished. Why was there a concomitant reduction in the defiance? The answer is that by gaining some overall self-control through learning to modify his whining and complaining, he became more in charge of himself, of his emotional responses. He had internalized some of the limits placed on him. In addition, he and his parents were not in as much conflict in general, easing the tension and strife in the household.

Next, Gene's parents used the same strategies used for modifying the whining and complaining to deal with his demanding behavior, which they had noticed during the observation period. For Gene this was mostly a level-two behavior (the level depends on the child). In just a week or so, the demanding style was practically gone. Moreover, the defiance had further diminished. In fact, there had been only two defiant reactions from Gene all during that week.

Of course, your experience may not be as striking, but the majority of parents I have taught these procedures to have had very similar results. In all situations, the overall self-control of their children increased, and the defiance decreased.

More Strategies for Defiance

Suppose that you have a defiant or belligerent child and you have used the procedure just outlined. Although her arguing and demanding are much better, and the defiance has improved, it is still a problem. This is an ideal time to impose a logical consequence. As always, sit down with your child and explain the problem to her:

> "Ellie, you are doing much better with your arguing and demanding, and I really appreciate that. However, there is still a problem. You still yell at me quite a bit and sometimes threaten that you will never go to school again. This is not

an acceptable way to talk to your mom or me. I have been thinking about it, and from now on when this happens, you will _____." (Impose a consequence here, usually the loss of some privilege. It needs to be specific according to the wants and desires of each particular child.)

"I know this is going to be hard, and I really don't want you to lose this privilege, but this is the only way I can think of to solve this problem. If you lose your privilege, there will be a way to get it back. If you go the whole next day without yelling or threatening, you can have it back."

Give your child a chance to talk it over with you, but don't let her talk you out of your strategy. If, in the course of the conversation, she starts yelling right then and there, impose the consequence. Stay calm and later approach her, telling her that if she doesn't yell the rest of the day, she can have her privilege back. Often this is the perfect time to do some modeling for her of the style you want instead of the defiance and yelling. By now I am sure you can do this quite well. Be sure to acknowledge and encourage her for the desired behavior.

Here is a summary of strategies for defiance:

1. Change the easiest oppositional styles first.
2. If any defiance remains, use logical consequences, and give your child a chance to redeem himself or herself.
3. Use modeling and rewards to elicit the style you want.

A Few Words about Tantrums

Tantrum! The very word makes most of us shudder. Images of children yelling and screaming, and flinging themselves to the ground flood our minds. In despair and desperation, parents pray for the two's to end: "Please, God. I'll do anything."

Tantrums during the twos, which range from roughly eighteen months to the early threes, are, of course, natural; they are to be expected. Nonetheless, knowing it doesn't help a bit. You still have to survive this period. Tantrums are an important part of your child's early psychological development. It is the child's attempt, albeit crude from our vantage point, to break away and achieve his or her first taste of independence. "No!" he screams, falling to the floor, legs churning. These kind of tantrums are genuine. They are an authentic expression of a two-year-old's emotions. They are the best that children can do during this time period, given their level of maturation.

There is not much you can do about tantrums at this stage of development. Wait them out. Try to redirect the child's behavior when it is over. And be nice to yourself. Special treats for yourself are in order. When our kids were this age, we found that getting away and going to the movies for an evening did wonders for our patience.

If your child is still having tantrums once this period is past, however, then something is amiss. The tantrums are no longer a genuine part of your child's emotional development and expression. They are now an attempt to manipulate you—to get you to give in to his or her whims and demands. As noted earlier, kids learn to be out of control because acting this way works. It gets them what they want.

All undesirable ways of relating, not just tantrums, are a manipulation, an attempt by the little darlings to force you into doing what they want. Of course, when kids are slamming doors and screaming, they are not such little darlings anymore. The fact that you want to lock them in the closet for a week is understandable (just don't do it). The bottom line is that you don't want to be coerced into doing what your child wants, whether it is through tantrums, arguing, belligerence, or any other undesirable style. If you give in, you are giving away your power, something you need and your child needs you to have.

As we have also seen, negative and oppositional styles can easily escalate, progressing from less intense ways of relating, such as whining and nagging, to much more intense ways, like screaming and breaking things. Rarely does a child just start with the latter behaviors, level four on our scale of emotional intensity. I've never heard of an eight-year-old suddenly throwing tantrums. It is always a progression of some sort.

Therefore, if your child does not outgrow the normal, but nonetheless harrowing, tantrums of the twos and is still having tantrums in the late threes and beyond, you need ways to deal with the problem. See the following Suggestion Box for some solutions.

How to Deal with Tantrums

---

1. Ignore children when they are out of control unless you, they, or the house is in danger or there is an emergency.

2. Take a parent timeout.

3. Discover the least intense oppositional style and work on changing that first.

"What kind of advice is he giving us?" you are probably wondering. "Why ignore them?" Well, what else can you do? The kid is out of control. No intervention in the world is going to work while he is writhing on the floor. If you pick him up, there will be some sort of a struggle and one of you may get hurt. Moreover, using physical force to control children is not a good idea (except in emergencies) because one day it won't work. It may not be for a year or five, but, believe me, the day will come. Then what will you do? So you don't want to get in the habit now. Therefore, as long as it's safe, walk away; although I would recommend that you keep an eye on him or her from a distance. But let the child have the tantrum in peace.

As soon as possible, take a parent timeout. Take a few deep breaths, have some chocolate, and regroup. Don't let tantrums overwhelm and depress you. They may be discouraging and draining, but there *is* something you can do.

Use the Same Old Strategy for Tantrums

You can help your child gain some self-control. Once again, observe the child to discover her least intense oppositional style, the one that will be the easiest to help her with. And start a new program (just like the one recommended for defiance). As stated previously, ignore the tantrums as much as you can for now.

As previously discussed, your child will gain some self-control if you modify less intense negative stylistic responses first. Next, as recommended for defiance, institute a logical consequence, usually a loss of a privilege, for the tantrums. Be sure, however, to do this only after the child has gained some self-control through dealing with the least intense styles first. And you can reinstate the privilege when there are no tantrums the following day. Be sure to use plenty of acknowledgement for improvements, and throw in a bonus or two as the behavior improves.

One parent made the following rule: "No tantrums in the house. All tantrums must be conducted outside—front yard or back. It's your choice." She made a recording on a tape player, and when her child started having the tantrum, she turned up the volume, and it boomed: **NO TANTRUMS IN THE HOUSE! ALL TANTRUMS MUST BE CONDUCTED OUTSIDE!** This so startled her child that the tantrums soon ended. I doubt that this will work in every case, but I would encourage you to be creative.

One final thought: Try to follow the general principles recommended; however, there is no need to follow them blindly or rigidly. Your child and your situation are unique. You will find some strategies that work that are not mentioned here. By all means, use them. In the end, you know best!

One more final thought: You can and will help your child end the tantrums and gain self-control.

CHAPTER SEVEN

Chores and Homework: "I Just Want to Play"

I've never met a child who couldn't wait to do chores and homework. But do them they must. These are the main responsibilities of childhood, and they are a training ground for the responsibilities of adulthood. This is why chores and homework are grouped together in this chapter. They require the same response from a child, the ability to put aside what they want in the moment in order to accomplish something in the long run.

CHORES

"Conrad won't do anything around the house," declared Mary Jane about her nine-year-old during a discussion in a parenting class. "When I ask him to do something such as clearing the table after dinner, he says he can't. He has to do his homework or call a friend. I end up doing everything." When asked how she felt about it, Mary Jane admitted she was resentful and that it was getting in the way of her relationship with her son.

By no means is this an unusual situation. A surprising number of parents have difficulties getting their children to do chores around the house. If this is your situation, ask yourself these questions:

1. Are the chores set up clearly?
2. Are your expectations appropriate?
3. Are there consequences?

1. *Are the chores clear to your children?* As stated in Chapter Three, be specific. Do your kids understand what, when, and how? Do they know exactly *what* you expect them to do? Do they know *when* they are expected to do it? Do they know *how* you expect them to do it? If the answers to these questions are not clear to your children, you can run into problems.

   Sit down with your children and go over their chores and responsibilities with them. Lay the details out clearly, and write them down. Post them in an obvious place such as the refrigerator door or a bulletin board, if you have one. Enlist their cooperation by letting them have input and by listening to their suggestions. They will feel better about chores when they are listened to, and they will feel like they are making important contributions to family life—and they are. Some things may be negotiable, such as who takes out the garbage or when a room is to be cleaned. Cleaning the room itself, however, should not be negotiable.

   Explain carefully to them how you want them to do things. Be sure you are clear, and ask them if they have questions. If something is not clear, use the modeling idea and demonstrate for them how you want it done. For example, it is worth the effort to clean their rooms with them the first time so that there can be no uncertainties in their minds about what it is that you expect.

Finally, be sure they know when you expect chores to be done. "Your room must be cleaned by noon on Saturday." "The trash must be emptied each evening after the dishes are done." If these things are vague, kids, like the little lawyers they can be, will find loopholes to escape through.

2. *Are your expectations age appropriate and are they reasonable?* Being reasonable means two things: Are they reasonable for your children and are they reasonable for you?

"Reasonable" for your kids means that you do not expect too much. After all, children do need to play. Other factors can also place demands on children. A nine-year-old was balking at his chores. When his mother described his chores to one of my classes, at first they seemed reasonable; but it turned out that there were other expectations. The child was taking piano and karate lessons, and playing baseball and soccer. When I asked, "When does he play?" she looked puzzled. She quickly saw that her child had hardly any free time. Unfortunately, in this society, with all its opportunities, this is an easy trap to fall into. Yet, children need free time in which they can explore, imagine, invent, and play with their friends.

"Reasonable" for you means that your children do have some chores. If they have none or hardly any, this is not reasonable for you because you do not get the help you need. The potential problem here is low expectations, being too easygoing and permissive. Often when children balk and resist doing tasks and chores when requested, they do so because they have not been expected to do much to begin with. They have not built up a chore muscle, so to speak, and thus are not amenable to, raking the leaves for example. Like any muscle-building endeavor, it takes practice to produce strength. Be sure they have enough practice so that they develop chore muscles.

3. *Are there consequences?* Corinne and Frank came to see me about their daughter, twelve-year-old Connie, who was out of control. She was running around with an undesirable crowd and coming and going as she pleased; she generally paid no heed to her parents' rules. She was also sassy and defiant. While there were several reasons for these problems, one of the main ones was that Corinne and Frank placed absolutely no consequences on her behavior. When I asked them about how they handled it when she went out all day Saturday without doing her chores, they said they told her not to do it.

It turned out that Corinne and Frank had never required much of Connie and had never imposed consequences on her. Therefore, they had no power over her, and she was out of their control. This problem did not start in her preteens. It started long before; however, now it was a major problem because Connie did not have the inner controls she needed.

When you set up your expectations and requirements for your children's chores, you must also have clear and appropriate consequences attached to them. This is where your power is. As stated previously, you control the consequences. Power is not about being bigger or stronger or tougher. It comes from imposing consequences, and imposing them consistently.

Introducing Changes: Building Chore Muscles

Obviously, it is easy for kids to adapt when you reduce your expectations and lower the demands on them. You are not going to encounter resistance: "C'mon Mom, I need more chores." *You* may find it hard to lower your expectations, but they won't.

The challenges come when you raise your expectations. Therefore, don't flood them with new requirements all at once. You have to build their chore muscles slowly, raising your requirements step-by-step, just as you do in the gym. You don't start out lifting heavy weights. You work up to it. Use the same principle in introducing chores to your kids.

Have a plan in mind and know what you want your child to do eventually. Then slowly, over a period of several weeks or even months, introduce the new chores one at a time. Give the kids time to work out their resistance and to adjust.

Be sure that the requirements and consequences are clear. Talk this out with them, so that they understand what is happening. Of course, they won't like it; but explain to them why it is important.

The most effective consequences are those that are tied closely to the issue. You can set it up like this: "When you finish cleaning your room on Saturdays, you may go out to play." (Remember the Saturday morning soccer game?) Then stick to your requirements. Be consistent and don't make exceptions, especially at the beginning.

Finally, if you run into oppositional styles along the way, deal with them first.

HOMEWORK

"April won't do her homework," said Eleanor. "She is falling way behind in spelling and math. And I can't make her do it."

This is a scenario I have heard countless times—the story of children who resist, balk, and sometimes just flat-out refuse to complete their projects and turn in assignments. Almost always, it is a symptom.

Rarely does a child who has chores and responsibilities at home not do his or her homework. Most of the time, excluding any learning problems or something like attention deficit disorder, children who balk at homework have not built up their chore muscle. From the parents' perspective, they are encountering a sudden problem. But like so many other issues we have discussed, it is not sudden. The real problem simply has been overlooked. Children who do not do their homework are the ones who either have no chores at home or who are regularly able to elude them. For April, in addition to refusing to do her homework, she was rude and defiant and terrorized her younger brother.

The remedy is to change her oppositional style and introduce chores. When these problems improve, then and only then should Eleanor deal with the homework issue. Often parents will find "spontaneous" improvement in the homework department, a result of developing a chore muscle, which then generalizes to include homework.

However, since this generalization does not always happen, at least not right away, parents need some other strategies for homework. There is an important issue to look at first, however. Homework is an emotionally loaded issue for most parents and understandably so. Parents want their children to succeed, and when a child falls behind in school, especially when it is due to resisting homework, parents become upset. They are afraid of the long-term consequences and often become angry with their child. These feelings are all okay, but do not let them get in the way. You need to remain calm with your child so that the relationship is not damaged and the bond between you and your child remains solid. When a child knows that her parents are behind her, even though she is messing up, it is much easier for her to make the needed changes.

Homework is your child's responsibility, not yours. Therefore, do not take it on. It is a matter between your child and her teacher. Therefore, a child needs to be accountable primarily to her teacher, not to her parent. This does not mean that you should not get involved. Just be sure the responsibility and accountability dimensions are clear to you.

Most teachers have good ideas and strategies for dealing with homework. Your job is to assist the teacher in any way you can. For example, the teacher may ask your child to write down her assignments on a piece of paper and to make sure it is signed by the teacher before the child goes home. Then you sign the paper indicating that you have seen it. That may be all that you need to do. Your child then knows that you know, and, thus, does her homework. Hopefully, it will be that easy.

The teacher may also suggest that you set up a regular time for your child to do her homework—the hour before dinnertime, for instance. Your job is to see that this happens. You can attach consequences to it: "When you finish your homework, you may watch TV (or talk to your friends on the phone)." This is the best you can do. If the homework is still not completed, let her teacher deal with it. Don't go into a frenzy about it with your child. Remember, you are only the teacher's assistant here. Your main task is to see that your child does her chores at home.

You must also understand that there are some things you just cannot do. You cannot make a child eat, and you cannot make a child learn. You can set up conditions that will maximize the likelihood that a child will eat and learn, but you cannot force these events. So set up the conditions in an alliance with the teacher. Impose appropriate consequences, let go of inappropriate objectives—such as trying to make your child learn—and be patient. Sooner or later your child will come around, particularly if you and she relate well and she has suitable chores at home.

CHAPTER EIGHT

Late Times and Bedtimes: Time-Related Misdemeanors

*I*t is not difficult to have endless power struggles with children around time: going to bed on time, getting up on time, getting to school on time, and getting home on time. Like time itself, these struggles can seem to go on eternally. They often start with the little ones doing the bedtime shuffle and continue with teenagers ignoring their curfew. In this chapter, lateness and bedtime will be specifically addressed, and you will, thereafter, be able to deal with any time-related misdemeanor.

LATE TIMES, OR MY HOW TIME FLIES

The Culbersons eat dinner at six o'clock each evening. For the third time in one week, Troy was late for the meal—ten minutes the first time, fifteen the second, and twenty-five the third time. Understandably, his parents were upset.

On the first occasion, Troy told his parents: "Steve got a flat tire and we had to carry his bike to his house." The other two times he offered another excuse, an old favorite: "I didn't know what time it was." He probably didn't, but he must learn to know the time. As children get older, they need to become responsible about time. They need to know what time it is so that they can follow rules and meet their obligations.

Here is what to do with a child who is habitually late for a meal: First, eat at your regular time. Don't wait dinner for the late child. Second, let the fish-and-chips fall where they may. If she comes in during dinner and the food is cold, then she gets a cold dinner (a natural consequence). If she complains, you can say, "When you come home on time, your dinner will be warm." If she is so late that dinner is over, then she misses her dinner—another natural consequence—and she doesn't get to snack on candy, chips, and ice cream. Of course, you talk to her in advance so that she knows what the consequences will be.

These consequences are powerful because they follow directly from her behavior; and, although they may take a few applications, they will work. If going without dinner seems too cruel, however, then create other consequences. You could have her clean up after dinner and do the dishes (assuming, of course, that it is not her job to begin with).

Another reason kids are late, besides having too good a time to stop playing, is that they don't want to do a task, such as a chore or their homework. Therefore, a different strategy must be used when Troy, who is supposed to be home at five o'clock to do his homework, does not show up on time. His parents may let him go without dinner once or twice to teach him to be on time; but, obviously, they'll have to use a different strategy (see next section) to get him to come home to do his homework.

TIME BANKS

An effective strategy that I like to use in many situations that involve problems with time is the creation of time banks. Time banks are especially useful when a child is late in taking care of a responsibility, such as a chore or homework. Time banks work like this: Each week Troy receives so much playtime to be with his friends—two hours a day during the week and ten hours on the weekend, for a total of twenty hours. This is put into his playtime bank.

Next, Troy's parents sit down with him and make out a chart with credits on one side and debits on the other. Each week he starts with the twenty hours of playtime. If he is on time all week, he gets his twenty hours of playtime. Whenever Troy is late, however, he loses playtime equal to the amount of time he has been late. Troy's mother or father sits down with him, and together they subtract that amount of time from his playtime. Troy should pay this debt right away, the following day if possible.

For example, if Troy arrives home at 5:30 instead of 5:00, he must pay back the thirty minutes out of his time bank. Therefore, the next day he must be home at 4:30. If the following day, he is late again and comes in at 5:00 instead of 4:30, he loses still another thirty minutes of his playtime. This means the next day he must be home by 4:00. Usually a couple of times will convince a child that lateness is a dead end. If it happens a third time, his parents still have a couple of options. They can double the amount of time he loses (if he is twenty minutes late, he loses forty minutes). Or they can institute a new rule: He must now do his homework before going out to play.

Sometimes resisting is more important to children than the consequences when you start a program like this. Kids are determined to win the power struggle about what time they should be home. Stick to your guns, and don't get into an argument about it. Let the consequences do their work. It may turn out that your child must stay in for a whole afternoon or even a whole Saturday. It won't shatter them. Kids will get the message, especially if you don't engage in a verbal power struggle.

Be sure to give children the opportunity to earn playtime back. In Troy's case, when he was on time three days in a row, he received a bonus of an hour of playtime credited to him in his bank.

CURFEWS

Time banks can also be used with older kids when they are not obeying their curfew. Suppose that your thirteen-year-old, who is allowed to go to her friend's on Friday and Saturday nights, must be home by 10:30, but generally is twenty to forty minutes late. Sit down with her and set up the time bank. The next time she is late, shorten her time to be home by the amount of time she is late. There is no need to argue with her or try to convince her to be home on time. The choice is clearly hers.

If she is still late, she may lose the privilege of being able to go to her friend's on the next evening that she would usually be allowed to go out. Down the line, when you find that she is consistently on time, you can "spontaneously" reward her by giving her a bonus, for example, extending the curfew on a given evening.

THE BEDTIME SHUFFLE

Kids should have regular bedtimes, whether they are three or thirteen. They should not be allowed to go to bed when they decide that they are tired, because most kids don't know when they are tired or will simply pretend they are not, especially when they want to do something such as watch a program on TV. It's 11:45. "Are you tired, Timmy?" "Oh, no." Timmy is seven. With older children, of course, you can be more flexible. To prevent bedtime problems, see the following Suggestion Box.

Prevent Bedtime Problems

From the very beginning, establish a set bedtime and a routine. For example, give children a fifteen-minute warning that bedtime is approaching, have them brush their teeth, and read to them for five or ten minutes. If you start this routine about the seventh month of pregnancy, you should have few bedtime problems.

Several time problems can arise around going to bed. We'll take each one in turn.

1. *Not being ready for bed on time.* If bedtime is 8:30 and at 8:55 Kirk is lying on his bed reading a comic book, here is what you can do: Use the time bank idea. Simply subtract the number of minutes Kirk goes past his bedtime from the next night's bedtime. This means that the next night's bedtime for Kirk is 8:05. When Kirk finds himself in bed at 6:30, he will probably get the message about bedtime. If Kirk likes to read, another strategy you can use is to allow him to read if he is ready on time.

2. *The shuffle.* The bedtime shuffle occurs when, after lights-out, children come wandering out because they need a drink of water, because their ear lobes hurt, or because there are forty-two monsters in their room. The little darlings truly believe that they are the first children ever to invent these excuses. Of course, the first couple of times this occurs, take your child's concerns seriously. However, you don't want these ploys to become devices to shuffle in and out of bed for half the night.

    The main strategy entails not rewarding the shuffle. When you talk over pains and monsters night after night, you are providing attention for this behavior. After you are sure that there are no real pains, have a pain check before lights-out for a few nights. No pains before the lights go out means no pains after the lights go out. To deal with monsters, you can do a monster sweep to show there are none lurking. Indicate that you will also check the room five minutes after lights-out, and say that if the monsters aren't there by then, they will not be there for that evening.

Moreover, if you have three nights in a row with no monsters, it means that they will never come to your house. Finally, make clear rules for bedtime. Getting up for water is not allowed, and enforce the rule with appropriate consequences.

A word of caution is needed: Sometimes at bedtime children are looking for attention because they really are not getting enough of it. Because the younger ones do not know how to express this need, they find other ways to, such as the bedtime shuffle. These days, with everyone so busy in our somewhat manic society and with the tremendous demands on parents, many children do not get enough time and attention from their parents. So do a little assessment, and be sure that your children are getting enough attention from you. It is the fuel that makes their engines run.

3. *Not getting up on time.* Kirk now has another problem, or his parents do, depending on how you look at it. They wake him or his alarm goes off, but he is still sleeping twenty-five minutes later. The race is on. Will he make the school bus? Will he get to school on time and where are his books anyway? The whole house is in a panic. What a wonderful way to start the day! Here is what to do if you have this problem:

First, let the problem be between Kirk and the school. Perhaps he will have detention when he is late. If the school does not have any sanctions, meet with his teacher and encourage her to institute some.

Second, don't rescue him morning after morning. Do not drive him to school. Let him walk. If it is a long way, and you are concerned about the distance

---

Use Time Banks to Help Kids Get Up

Use the same principle we have been using with lateness and not being ready for bed on time. If a child is supposed to get up at 7:00 and she gets up at 7:20, she owes the time bank twenty minutes and, therefore, must go to bed twenty minutes earlier that night. "When you get up on time, you may go to bed at your regular hour." When she gets up on time for a few days in a row, reward her on the weekend with a later bedtime or a sleep-in.

---

or his safety, you can drive him part of the way and let him walk the rest of the way, while you drive along beside him; and yes, it is a shame that it's snowing this morning.

Third, even though I have just stated that the problem is between Kirk and the school, there is something you can do, especially when you have to be out of the house at a certain time: Once again, use a time bank. (See the Suggestion Box above.)

Finally, when time is the problem, time is your leverage. When kids are late or won't go to bed or won't get up, they want more time for one thing or another. And you control the allotment of their time. Therefore, you can use it as a consequence to help them be responsible. Happy dreams!

CHAPTER NINE

Ignoring, Broken Promises, and Excuses: Kids' Curve Balls

Children are smart, and because they are, they can be quite adept at finding ways to outwit their parents. This chapter examines three of the ploys children use to try to throw you off balance in order to get their way. It's easy to swing and miss when they throw you these curve balls.

The Basic Strategy for Handling Kids' Curve Balls

1. Learn to identify what your child does that *interferes* with cooperation.

2. Deal with that issue first.

IGNORING: THE NO-RESPONSE RESPONSE

"Sarah," Mom calls. "Please pick up the toys in the living room."

No response.

"Sarah."

Dead silence.

"Sarah, did you hear me?"

All remains quiet on the ranchero.

"Sarah? Answer me now."
The silence continues to thunder through the house.

"Sarah," Mom calls.

No response.

"Sarah, come and get your allowance."

Zip! Sarah sets a new speed record from her room to the kitchen.

About five minutes after humans discovered speech, kids invented what has become a perennial favorite, the no-response response: Don't answer, don't look up, and pretend you're deaf. Some four thousand generations of children have now used this approach; it's just as effective in the age of technology as it was in the age of the Neanderthal. Ignoring parents is a powerful weapon in a child's arsenal of resistance, and I don't know any parents who don't get at least a little aggravated when they are not responded to, especially when it is a regular occurrence.

Most of the time kids adopt the no-response tactic when they know or suspect that you want them to do something. Even if you just call their name without saying anything else, chances are pretty good that they know from the subtle tone in your voice (and sometimes not so subtle) that a request is in the mail. It goes without saying that before you can get children to do something, you must get their attention. Their ignoring you says, "You don't have my attention, and, therefore, I don't have to do what you want." When this succeeds, guess who has the power?

Yelling and becoming frustrated are common reactions to this ploy, but usually they have little effect. On the other hand, you do not want to ignore the ignoring behavior, either by pretending it doesn't exist or by trying to go around it (for example, repeating your direction over and over again). This just leads to more frustration.

The Suggestion Box at the beginning of this chapter offers a general principle that can guide you in this situation. *Deal with whatever interferes with cooperation first.* What interferes is any ploy or strategy to avoid chores or limits. This is the same strategy we have used in regard to oppositional styles.

Ignoring, or the no-response response, is one such ploy that interferes with cooperation. First, deal with it as a separate issue. In the situation with Sarah, her mother should identify and single out the ignoring as the problem to be dealt with, before trying to get her to follow any directions.

When you run into this problem, assuming your child does not have any kind of hearing problem, ask whether or not he or she heard you. Then make this rule: "When I talk to you, you must answer me, or there will be a consequence." Be sure that you set up the consequence with your child in advance, a consequence that is related to speech, or the lack of it—for example, the child will not be allowed to make any requests to you for some period of time, say a couple of hours. Then, if a friend should call and ask her to come over to her house, she can't go because she can't ask.

Then, the next time you run across the no-response tactic, go up to your child and put your hand gently on her shoulder. This makes it almost impossible for her to ignore you because the automatic response to touch is to look up. Remind her of the rule about responding when talked to, and give her the choice of either responding or dealing with the consequence. Be sure to tell her, though, that the next time the consequence will go into effect automatically when she doesn't respond. This way you won't have to chase her down to get a response.

Don't start this way:

> "Sarah, did you hear me?"
> "No."

It gives Sarah the chance to pretend that she is deaf and will easily lead to an argument about whether or not she heard you. Try this instead:

> "Sarah, you didn't answer me when I called."
> "Mnn." (Imagine the most noncommittal response possible.)
> "What is the rule about not responding when I speak to you?"
> "I can't ask you for anything, unless it's an emergency, for two hours."
> "That's right. That goes into effect right now." Mom looks at her watch. "The no-request period will end at 5:15. Now please pick up the toys in the living room."

Promote the behavior you want. And don't forget to acknowledge and encourage her when she does respond to you.

BROKEN PROMISES: "I'LL DO IT IN A MINUTE"

> "Jeremy, please come downstairs. I want you to take out the garbage."
> "Okay, Mom, I'll be down in one minute."

Ten minutes go by. Suddenly, Mom realizes that Jeremy is way past his estimated time of arrival and that the garbage hasn't budged from under the sink. In this situation, Jeremy didn't ignore his mother. In fact, he agreed to her request, but then didn't follow through. He didn't do what he said he would do. He broke his promise.

Although this strategy is a common way for kids to avoid responsibilities, no one taught it to Jeremy. Each ploy kids use to "get out of" what they are supposed to do is a creative piece of work—a child's very own invention. If only this creativity could be used to solve the world's problems!

How do you handle it when a child agrees and then doesn't follow through, when he says one thing and does another? The natural reaction is to try to make him comply, the old enforcer parenting role. But the best approach is to deal with the whole piece, namely, that Jeremy said he would cooperate but did not.

Some brief instruction is in order:

> "Jeremy, it is very important for you to do what you say you are going to do. If you don't want to take out the garbage, then tell me. If you have a good reason, perhaps it can wait. But don't get into the habit of saying that you will do something and then not do it."

To remedy this situation, start by using interpersonal rewards. Acknowledge him for doing what he says he will do. Make a big point of it, because one way children learn integrity is by keeping their agreements with you. You might even say that keeping agreements and keeping one's word are the cornerstone of integrity. In this sense every little agreement is important because it involves this issue. It's an old adage but a truly vital one: A person's word is their most valuable possession.

Be sure that *you* follow through to see that your child follows through when he makes these little agreements with you, such as, "I'll do it in a minute." If interpersonal rewards don't get the job done, you can always introduce a logical consequence.

For example, Jeremy promises that he will do his homework right after dinner if he can first go over to Tommy's to see his new bike. You agree. About thirty minutes after dinner you notice that Jeremy is in his room putting together a model airplane. A possible consequence in this situation is to take away the airplane, making sure that he understands that it is not only because he is not doing his homework but also because he has not kept his agreement.

EXCUSES: "I FORGOT"

"I forgot to mow the lawn."
"I can't do my homework cuz' I forgot my books."
"I forgot my uniform."
"I forgot to put my bike away."

At some point in their lives most kids come up with some of these excuses. "After all," they figure, "if I didn't remember, it's not my fault. I can't help it." After the first time or two, however, forgetting should be an expensive proposition for a child.

The best way to deal with forgetting behavior is to use natural and logical consequences. Let's look at each of the four "I forgot" excuses.

Forgetting to do a chore, such as mowing the lawn, requires a logical consequence. In this and the following examples, after the first time it happens, let your child know that forgetting is not an acceptable excuse and the next time there will be a consequence for forgetting. Tell her what that consequence will be. In addition, the forgotten chore, such as mowing the lawn, should be done immediately.

Forgetting to bring home books from school can be a little tricky to handle. We briefly discussed this in regard to Rachel in Chapter Four. Recall that her mother would take her to school to get her books, thus rewarding the "forgetful" behavior. This is a trap that parents can easily fall into because they want their children to be happy.

Your child needs her books so that she can study and do her homework. If you discover the forgotten books before her teacher has left for the day, she should go back to school to get them. Walking is the transportation of choice here. Therefore, Rachel should walk back to school to get her books. This is a natural consequence.

If, however, it is too far or she cannot make it to school before her teacher leaves, take her to school, if possible. The first time give her a free ride. After that, inform her that there will be a charge. Tell her that in the future it will cost her for the gas and taxi services that you are providing. Explain how much gas costs and what your services are worth per hour, and prorate it according to how much time is required to go to school, retrieve the books, and return home. (Obviously, you must not be excessive here.) After a couple of rides to school, she should get the idea as her pocketbook empties or her allowance disappears. Forgetting books will be a thing of the past.

What if the school is closed for the day and you can't retrieve the books? A logical consequence would be no playtime, no talking on the phone, and no watching TV when books are absent and homework can't be done. Allowing your child to do these things instead of homework rewards the undesired behavior. So remove these privileges, and in their place give her some homework exercises to do, such as practicing spelling or doing multiplication tables, things that you can easily make up. If the forgetting does not have a payoff, your child will soon forget to forget.

The third situation is one in which a child forgets something she needs and you get a frantic call saying, "I forgot my uniform for Brownies. Will you bring it over to Mrs. Jones's house right away?" Of course, we all forget sometimes, so the first time you might do this, but only the first time.

Let your child know that if it happens again, it is her problem to solve, that you are not going to make special trips for her, and that she will need to be more responsible. Then, let the natural consequence go into effect, whatever it is—in this case being at the meeting with no uniform.

The last situation to consider is the one in which a child offers the "I forgot" excuse as the reason why something undesirable happened, such as a bike being stolen. "I forgot to put it away last night." This means: "Therefore I am not responsible." There is no need to give a long lecture on the desirability of taking care of things. Instead, briefly explain that forgetting is not an excuse and that it is now his problem that he no longer has a bicycle. The natural consequence will be clear and more powerful than any words you can use.

The important thing is not to let your child find a way to excuse his or her way out of responsibility. If the excuses work, then kids have found a way to undermine your authority and avoid taking responsibility for their actions. You certainly don't want this to be a pattern that carries into their teens and adult lives.

CHAPTER TEN

Sibling Rivalry: When Harry Socked Sally

*T*he day that siblings don't fight will be the day I win the lottery. Just like everyone else, including husbands and wives, children are going to argue and fight with each other. When you live with someone day in and day out, there is bound to be conflict, and you are going to have disagreements. The challenge is to manage the conflict and disagreements so that life can proceed. A certain amount of dissension between siblings then is normal and to be expected. It becomes a concern when the fighting and arguing is constant, or one child gets physically hurt by another, or they haven't talked to each other in two years.

CAUSES

Besides the day-to-day friction that arises between people when they live together, there are other reasons that can be at the root of ongoing sibling rivalry. The first is that the older child hasn't gotten over the arrival of his sib. This can be an issue particularly when several years separate the children, but is by no means limited to this situation. The customary way to describe this event is that the older child feels displaced. What this really means, though, is that the older one feels less important and/or less loved.

In the excitement and the flurry of activity and changes accompanying the newborn's arrival, be sure that you don't overlook the needs of the older child. All the developmental books recommend that parents spend time with the older child and involve him or her in some care of the new one. And I strongly agree. This is good advice, but it places more demands on parents at a time when demands are already increased. So you must find a way to balance all of this.

There is no magical solution, but one thing that helps is to be sure that you have plenty of help. Don't try to do it all yourself. Support will enable you to have time for the new baby and for the older child. The older child will need his or her share of time and attention even more during the period of excitement about the new baby. In his or her world, this arrival is unsought, the excitement is ridiculous, and the baby is an unwelcome intrusion.

Another reason for ongoing rivalry is that one child may actually be favored. I know that we all love our children equally. Nevertheless, it is quite possible to favor one over the other. For example, occasionally one child has a special talent or is extremely bright and, as a result, may get a great deal of attention and praise, not only from parents but also from people in general. The other child may feel left out or even inadequate, either of which can lead to resentment toward his sib. Where else would he take out his frustrations?

The solution is to try to be aware of these and any other reasons for one child to be favored over another and to distribute the attention evenly. For example, if one child receives a great deal of attention for winning the county spelling bee, be sure that the other kids have opportunities to shine and sparkle in their own ways. Talk things over with them to see if they feel left out, and help them understand that they don't have to do anything special to be loved.

Sometimes an older child becomes upset and jealous of a younger sibling when the younger is allowed to do things that he or she wasn't allowed to do at the same age. This is especially so if the parents have made a notable shift in their child-rearing approach and have become less strict. The older child may take his frustration out on the younger one when in actuality he is angry with his parents.

STRATEGIES

Here are some tried-and-true strategies:

1. *Hold family meetings.* In Chapter Three the importance of family meetings was discussed. One purpose of family meetings can be to work out solutions to various kinds of family problems. Let your children express their feelings, no matter what they are. Promote sharing by helping them find ways to do that. If nothing else, these meetings can engender a sense of togetherness that can help lessen strife and conflict.

2. *Don't take sides.* It is a favorite ploy of kids to get their parents to take sides. When Harry socks Sally, naturally, it's easy to side with poor Sally, especially when she weighs twenty pounds less than Harry. Of course, hitting is not allowed, but in terms of who is responsible, it may be more complicated. Younger children can learn to be quite adept at playing victim, all the while setting up the older one to take the rap.

   Through her careful observations and analysis of Harry's personality, Sally, who aspired to become a forensic psychologist, knew that when she borrowed her brother's Nintendo without asking permission, he would become upset. To say that it gave her a certain diabolical delight is charitable. On the one hand, she didn't anticipate that her brother would sock her; but on the other, that gave her all the more reason to run to her mother with the shocking news: "Harry tried to kill me."

While you have to teach Harry that hitting is not a solution, it doesn't mean that he is the only one responsible for what happened. It is best to stay out of these conflicts, using the strategies mentioned to help them resolve their issues with each other. It is worth mentioning that even when the events unfold before your very eyes, you don't always know the total context; and, therefore, it is still dangerous to take sides.

3. *Separate them.* As much as siblings seem to hate each other, they also hate to be separated for very long. After a short time apart, either they genuinely miss each other (which they would never admit) or they miss menacing each other. In either case, being together should be considered a reward.

   Thus, when the fighting gets too bad, whatever that means for you, give them the consequence of separation: "You may not play with each other for the rest of the day" (or perhaps for two days). You could also cut off all communication for the day. They are not allowed to play with each other, and, in addition, they may not even talk to each other for the rest of the day. This consequence may encourage them to rethink their squabbling.

4. *Remove your attention.* There are occasions when the arguing and fighting is for your benefit. When my children were small and I thought this was the case, I would send them outdoors: "Go outside to have your fight," I would say. Or, "You can't fight inside, but you may fight outside. I don't want to listen to it." Sometimes this worked like magic. For some strange

reason, whatever was troubling them didn't matter anymore. Suddenly, the conflict was over.

5. *Help your children work out their differences.* This is not for young children, but when they get a little older, encourage talking and communication. The following Suggestion Box shows you how to help children negotiate and resolve conflict.

Teach Children How to Resolve Conflict

1. Have a cooling-off period.

2. Have each child state his or her case.

3. Then, have each repeat what the other said to see if it is accurate.

4. Next, have each tell how what the other child did makes him or her feel.

5. Help both children to understand that it is impossible for them to have what they want all the time.

6. Have them suggest solutions.

These six steps take practice on their part and patience on your part. Don't expect that they will easily resolve any differences, and don't do step six for your children; let them work it out.

SUMMARY

If your children are fighting excessively, check to see whether there are any underlying reasons and try to remove them. Otherwise, be sure that you do not reward the fighting with your attention and that you provide consequences for the undesired behavior. Keeping them apart in various ways and for varying amounts of time seems to work well.

CHAPTER ELEVEN

Dawdling, Procrastination, and Picky Eaters: 3-2-1, Mission Aborted

What is it about dawdling and procrastination that make parents want to tear their hair out? "I can't get him to get ready" is a standard lament of parents of dawdlers. Basically, these are problems in *not* doing something. A child is not ready on time for school, she doesn't eat her dinner, or she puts off a report until the last moment, and even then it may not get finished. These responses are usually labeled passive resistance. How do you get a child to stop *not* doing something?

The most important thing to keep in mind is that while dawdling, procrastination, and picky eating appear to be passive responses, they actually are not. These ploys are active responses that require some effort to put into play and keep in play. But they look otherwise on the surface, and that is why parents often want to scream in frustration as they attempt to get their children to do something.

THE FINE ART OF DAWDLING

Here is how the dictionary defines dawdling: (1) to waste time in trifling; (2) to loiter; (3) to move slowly and idly. It is a highly sophisticated type of resistance, which can be raised to an art form—the ability to appear to be engaged in a task and at the same time to be doing absolutely nothing. But it does take energy to appear to be engaged in that task.

Children have an uncanny way of manifesting this behavior when you are in a hurry or have an appointment or both. As you are rushing to get out the door to be on time for an appointment, your little dawdler is moving at a snail's pace, taking three minutes to put his socks on. Or, you may simply find him lying on his bed reading a comic book. Whatever the scenario, you can be sure that a quiet rebellion is taking place.

Wally described to me how his seven-year-old son, Nick, dawdled before his hockey games. He was supposed to have his uniform on before they left the house, but Nick would dawdle in his room, playing with his toys or staring out the window. Since he was seldom ready to leave on time, Wally and Nick would get into big arguments, with Wally ending up very frustrated.

The main trap for parents in these situations is to fall into a nagging style; and this is easy to do. Wally felt pressure because he did not want Nick to miss out on his game because he was the team coach and did not want to be late. It's easy to nag, urge, remind, cajole, implore, and otherwise drive ourselves loony when dealing with dawdling. These tactics seldom work, however, and make both parent and child even more frustrated.

Strategies

If you are having an ongoing problem with dawdling, first try a timer. Tell your child what time you must leave. Then set a timer to go off five or ten minutes before departure time. Sometimes this simple technique works, and children, especially younger ones, respond to the ring. You can reward them for responding with a hug or, occasionally, a special privilege. Unfortunately, however, this approach does not always work. Then, it is time to introduce some consequences.

The use of natural and logical consequences is the obvious solution. If a child is not dressed and ready to leave the house on time for a game, being left at home is a natural consequence. (The other parent stays home and watches him.)

However, because Wally was a single parent, he required a different solution. He used a logical consequence to deal with the problem. If not dressed when it was time to leave, Nick would have to sit on the sidelines and watch the game rather than play. This consequence was a big one for Nick, since he loved to play hockey; and it was not a particularly easy decision for Wally, because he was the coach of the team and played on a team himself. Hockey was an important part of his life.

Wally explained to Nick what the consequences would be if he was not dressed in time to leave for the game. The very next game Nick was not dressed at the departure time. He finished putting his hockey uniform on in the car.

> "I'm ready to play," Nick told his Dad when they arrived at the ice rink.
>
> "That's good that you got dressed in the car, Nick," Wally replied. "But you can't play today because you weren't ready when we left the house."
>
> Nick reacted vehemently, "Dad, I'm ready!"

Wally told Nick again that he could not play, and he stood his ground, even though Nick sulked on the bench for most of the game. After that, Nick was dressed in plenty of time for his games.

A more difficult situation is one in which a child is not ready for school. You can't say, "Well, you're not dressed, so you can't go to school today." Many children would be only too delighted at this consequence. Norma told me that she got so sick and tired of the fight to get Emily off to school each morning that on one occasion in sheer frustration she took her daughter to school in her pajamas. Norma had never heard of natural consequences, but this certainly was one, and it was a beauty. After that incident, Emily was dressed and ready to go to school.

You can't always use natural consequences. For example, they won't work when children are being taken to places they do not necessarily want to go, such as to the doctor. When these situations arise, use logical consequences. Avoid a verbal power struggle. Simply set up the consequence in advance, and when the requirement is not met, let the consequence do the talking.

One approach is to use the time bank idea. For example, for every minute she is not ready, she loses one, two, or three minutes of playtime. You may be late or even miss an appointment or two at first following this approach, but if you are consistent, it will work. The important thing is to set it up so that you do not have to nag or get into arguments and can let the consequences have their effect.

PROCRASTINATION: NOT A HABIT FOR KIDS TO GET INTO

Unlike dawdling, we don't need to turn to the dictionary for a definition of procrastination. We all know that it means to put off tasks until later, and we know it because we all do it once in a while. Although the occasional putting off of tasks is nothing to be concerned about, it is an easy pattern to fall into. When you notice your child is starting to procrastinate, intervene quickly before it becomes an entrenched habit. (Ask any adult who has this problem, and she will tell you how hard it is to change it.)

Suppose that Carlos is building a model airplane, which he is going to enter into a contest sponsored by his Cub Scout troop. He was given a month to build it, and with three days left to finish, he has just begun. When children put things off, parents can easily swing into the nagging style of parenting:

"Carlos, you have to get started on your model. You have only three days left."

Two hours later: "Carlos, you need to get started on your project." A certain urgency is now detectable in Mom's voice.

An hour later: "Carlos! When are you going to build your model? Time is running out." Panic is setting in; not with Carlos, of course, but with Mom.

It is truly difficult not to nag in these situations, and if you have a tendency to nag in general, then you may have to tape your mouth shut for a few days. I'm just kidding, of course. However, how do you handle this problem? Or is it a problem?

Basically, there are two kinds of situations that can occur in regard to procrastination. There are required tasks, ones that a child must perform, such as chores, homework, and agreements that he makes with others. And there are optional tasks, such as building the model airplane. The child is doing it only for himself. Here is a chart to show what your response should be in each situation:

	Intervention	*Consequence*
Required Tasks	Yes	Logical
Non-required Tasks	No	Natural

Carlos is building a model for Cub Scouts, but it is not a required task. Therefore, if he does not want to do it, he shouldn't have to, unless he has made an agreement with his leader or troop to do it. While it is desirable that he follow through when he says that he is going to do something, he is the only one who will be affected if he does not. No one else is depending on him to finish the project. Therefore, there is no need for parental intervention. Simply let the natural consequences, if there are any, play out. If Carlos does not finish his model on time, it will not be entered in the contest.He may or may not feel bad about it—the consequence may or may not affect him.

Here is a slightly different scenario: Those who complete the project get to go whale watching on an afternoon boat trip. If Carlos really wants to go on the trip but does not get his project finished, he loses out and is quite disappointed. This is a chance for a parent to point out briefly and gently the connection between procrastinating behavior and the consequence. Once pointed out, the parent can say, "I feel bad for you that you missed out. I hope you don't put it off next time." Thus, a natural consequence follows from the behavior, and there is no need for parental intervention.

Required tasks, such as chores or homework, usually demand parental intervention, which means a logical consequence. Suppose that Carlos has a history report due in three days and has not even started it. Another parenting style that can easily come into play, a variation on the pleaser, is that of the rescuer. Because Carlos's parents don't want him to suffer or fail, they rescue him. One of them sits down with him on the night before the report is due and practically writes it for him. As we have already seen several times, this only rewards the undesired behavior—the procrastination.

"Why should I put out all this effort? If I wait, Dad will help me," Carlos thinks. It won't be long until Carlos is lying out in the backyard, sipping a soft drink on his lounge chair while his parents do his homework. Not really, but you get the idea. Therefore, to prevent a premature life of leisure and possibly loafing, don't nag or rescue. See the following box for some suggestions on how to handle the situation.

How to Put an End to Putting Things Off

1. Explain the problem.

2. Help your child develop a plan for completing an assignment or a chore that she does not want to do.

3. Set up a logical consequence.

4. Acknowledge (reward) the desired behavior.

"I HATE CARROTS"

It's easy for kids to become choosy about what they will and will not eat, and this behavior can become another way to resist passively. If you don't start children off at an early age eating a wide variety of foods, the problem only gets tougher. Taste is an individual matter, and we can't expect kids to like everything that we put in front of them. However, if there is not one single vegetable that gets a ride to their stomachs, then something is wrong.

The main trap with the picky eater is to fall into a power struggle in which the parent tries to force the child to eat. A threatening or intimidating parental style emerges, while the child folds his arms and clenches his teeth. Few parents win the battle in this arena, and you may end up with a child who is determined to resist. Moreover, if it goes on too long or is too intense, real damage to the relationship may result. A different approach is called for.

It is highly distressing for parents when the only foods a child will eat are hamburgers and fries. I contribute to their fear when I suggest that if the child doesn't like what is being served, she doesn't eat. "NOT EAT!? What do you mean not eat? Do you want my child to starve?" Well, just a little. It's amazing how appetites change when one is really hungry. Perhaps, you've noticed that yourself. Food looks different and wonder of wonders, it tastes different—as in "better."

Suppose that your child refuses to eat the dinner you prepare and goes to bed hungry—without an after-dinner dessert or an

after-dinner snack. You are not being a mean parent, you are trying to solve an important problem. The next day the child will be
pretty hungry. Set a healthy meal in front of her, explaining that
she needs to try a few bites to see what she thinks. You will be surprised at the eventual response. Cautiously, most kids will put a
speck of food in their mouths, grimace, and then look like they are
going to throw up. At this point, take a deep breath. Once you get
by the initial reaction (providing you don't react), they will likely
try a bite or two and say: "Well, maybe it's not too bad." Or, "This
stuff is rotten, but I'll eat it."

Gradually, you can help them try more foods. Contrary to
what many people think, tastes can be cultivated, although you
have to be willing to proceed slowly and patiently.

Another way to approach the picky-eater problem is through the
use of foods they do like. One child I know of liked only hot dogs. It
was hot dogs for breakfast, hot dogs for lunch, and guess what for
dinner. If this is your situation, don't fret: all is not lost. The hot dog,
or any food a child likes, can be used as a reward for eating the
healthy foods that they don't like. To the hot-dog king or queen, just
say, "You can have a hot dog after you eat some vegetables." Of
course, there will be a protest, followed by "I'm not eating that stuff."

You might say: "Very well, then, don't eat. But when you do eat
your vegetables, you can have your hot dog." You get back to the bottom line: They have a choice to eat what you serve or to not eat at all.

If they go to bed hungry, so be it. It is not the end of the world!
And soon the picky-eating game will end. Plan this carefully, and at
first try to serve them something that you suspect they may secretly
like. For example, they might really like carrots but because winning
the power struggle around food has become so important, they won't
tell you. However, it is critical for their health that they relinquish
their "addiction" to hot dogs or whatever their food of "poison" is.

Whatever you do, don't try to use force. It simply creates too
much tension and dissension. Let them face the consequences
for their actions. A few hours of hunger will awaken them to a
new world of taste and end the power struggle around eating.

CHAPTER TWELVE

Carelessness and Sloppiness: Sloppy Joes and Marys and "Careless-itis"

*T*here is a certain malady with different strains that people of all ages can get infected by, and it is one that usually originates sometime in childhood. The two strains of this disease manifest as messiness and carelessness with one's own and sometimes others' possessions. Moreover, these afflictions usually have a large impact on other people, which the person with these maladies seems to be completely oblivious to.

"CARELESS-ITIS"

It had just stopped raining when Ed went out to the garage to get a tool. As he crossed the driveway, he saw his son Jeffrey's schoolbooks lying in a puddle near the garage door.

> "How many times have I told that kid to be careful," Ed fumed, remembering that only last week Jeffrey had lost his new jacket, the one he had begged his parents for and just had to have.

"I don't know what to do with Jeffrey," Ed told his wife Jan. "He is going to put us in the poorhouse."

Jeffrey has developed a case of "careless-itis," a condition in which the "victim" of this malady has lost the ability to care for his possessions and keep them in reasonably good condition. Various properties of the victim are often damaged and in poor repair. On top of that, the victim's possessions sometimes suddenly disappear. "Careless-itis" may have a sudden onset, but more likely, it develops gradually over a period of months or even years.

This condition can be extremely expensive to the parents of the victim, who not only must purchase and re-purchase clothing, toys, sports equipment, hair ribbons, cosmetic jewelry, and numerous other items, but may also require frequent visits to a psychotherapist. However, I recommend natural and logical consequences to treat this condition.

Lost Possessions

If a child loses an item, he or she either goes without it or must pay for its replacement. (We are discussing habitual problems here, not a first occurrence.) If a child does not need the item, such as a decorative scarf, bicycle, or baseball bat, then she can simply wait until she has saved enough money to replace it. If she does not wish to replace it, allow her to make that choice. As she loses more and more of her possessions, she will eventually feel the impact of not having them and will want to do something about it. At that point, you can help her to take responsibility for her behavior and devise a plan to replace the items she wants. Under no circumstances is it advisable for you to pay for the items.

I would discourage loans, which would enable her to have the item immediately but pay for it later. Besides, many parents find that recouping the loan becomes a struggle and results in considerable emotional upset.

If the lost items are a necessity, such as schoolbooks or a warm winter coat, you have no choice but to replace them immediately. In this case, you will have to put up the money, but it should be your child's responsibility to repay you for them. This is a logical consequence, which you impose. You can deduct a portion of their allowance every week (it is not a good idea to take their whole allowance away; leave them something), and/or you can have them do extra chores to earn some additional money to pay you back; but don't let them earn the money too quickly. Let it go on for a while so that they can feel the consequences. This strategy is not meant to be punitive. It is just that you don't want them to get off the hook too easily. Let them feel the burden of repaying.

Poor Care of Possessions

Another irritant for parents occurs when possessions are not cared for. Common examples are torn clothes and broken toys. Use the same principles just mentioned to cure this habit. Let them pay for damages or go without. These are the consequences that result from their actions. By all means, don't reward the behavior by replacing something because you feel sorry for them. Let them struggle a bit. Again, this is not meant to be punitive or mean. It is aimed at helping them learn to be responsible. The following Suggestion Box contains a chart that shows how to deal with this issue.

Guidelines for Handling "Careless-itis"		
	Intervention	*Consequence*
Necessary Items	Yes	Logical
Non-necessary Items	No	Natural

If unchecked, careless-itis has long-term consequences that can make a person's life difficult in adulthood. This can range from simply having to spend considerably more money than would otherwise be necessary because possessions are easily lost, damaged, and broken to having the people living with the careless individual be frequently or perhaps continually angry about the problem, because it often spreads to damaging and losing other people's possessions as well.

Moreover, it easily leads to a general lack of awareness about the value of money and possessions. For example, I know someone who bought an old house and neglected to care for it, not through any malice, but simply because it did not occur to him. This lack of awareness eventually resulted in a large financial loss, because when he went to sell it, the house required a tremendous amount of extra work.

All children are occasionally going to lose or damage things. Talk with them about it, and help them understand the value of money and caring for their possessions. If, on the other hand, the problem becomes habitual and you have an "itis" on your hands, use the remedies suggested. They will last a lifetime.

SLOPPY JOES AND MARYS

Remember those roommates you had who were such a pain to live with? You'd find their clothes scattered all over the apartment, the not-quite-empty pizza box hanging off the TV, and the dishes in the sink so encrusted you'd swear they were about to lift off. Perhaps, even more painfully, you remember that you cleaned up after them a few times, too. Remember how much fun that was?

Well, you don't want a repeat, because sloppy, messy kids can be a pain, too. The habit of untidiness is a close cousin to "careless-itis," but it stands on its own merits (or demerits as the case may require).

I have heard many, many parents complain that their kids' rooms are an impenetrable jungle, that they leave their toys and clothes strewn about the house, and that they just can't get them to pick up and put away their belongings. The solution, however, is fairly simple: "If you drop it or leave it, you lose it."

Have clear rules and guidelines about the "state of the house." You should be clear about where your children can and cannot leave their possessions. For example, you may not care about how the family room is kept on a daily basis, but you may care about the rest of the house. You may require that the family room be picked up only once a week, but the rest of the house be picked up every day. You may require that toys, clothes, and so on not be left in the entryway and the living room. Whatever your rules are, be sure they are clear.

Then, whenever the kids drop items in forbidden places or leave them lying around, you confiscate them and put them away for a specified period of time. Usually, a few days is reasonable. This can be tough at times, for example, when Joe or Mary needs to bring the item to a scout or brownie meeting. But you need to be tough once in awhile. We've seen this principle many times. It promotes fast learning. Remember that you are tough—as in firm—about the issue and gentle in your style.

Another situation occurs when the item left around is something that the child has no inherent interest in. He doesn't care if you take it away. This could be a dirty dish left in the family room or even a pair of shoes. Suppose that Joe leaves a dirty glass in the family room. You could handle it by not allowing him to drink sodas anywhere in the house except the kitchen, or he might lose his privilege of having sodas and be forced to drink water, of all things. Just use logical and natural consequences, as discussed in Chapter Four, and you will avoid the sloppy Joe and Mary syndrome.

A touchy issue, especially for teens, is how clean and picked up they should keep their rooms. "It's my room," (as in territory) "and I'll keep it the way I want to," declares the desperately-searching-for-independence teen. He has a point. After all, it is his room. Most of the time, this situation can be avoided by training children from a young age to be tidy. In the long and, especially, the short run, life goes better for everyone.

Prevention of Messiness Is the Best Cure

Don't wait! Train children from an early age to pick up after themselves and to be tidy. (You will also cure the headaches you won't be getting.)

WHAT'S YOURS IS MINE, TOO

One of the strategies that I recommend is to give rewards for the behavior you want. Acknowledge kids; give them an extra reward in the form of a bonus. Since you have made it thus far in this book, here is a bonus for you. I am throwing in some extra advice about a situation that is not listed in the Table of Contents. I know that I don't have to do it, but since you have been such loyal readers, here it is. It involves respecting each other's personal space.

Ellen comes tearing down the stairs yelling, "Mom, Shannon is wearing my earrings. Tell her to take them off."

Jeff walks into the garage and takes a wrench from the rack. To this day, its location remains a mystery.

Carrie barges into her parents' bedroom without bothering to knock.

These children don't pay attention to where another person's space and possessions stop and where their own begin. They all have some "boundary issues."

Members of a family are entitled to their possessions, their privacy, and their own space, even if, when sharing a room, it's only a bed and part of a closet. Nothing can raise the ire of another person in the family more than not having his or her possessions and space respected and valued. It is absolutely essential, therefore, for families to have clear rules about this.

This issue becomes difficult to deal with because often it isn't noticed until it looms quite large. The problem starts with little things, such as small intrusions into another's space or borrowing a pencil without asking. From there it slowly escalates. The three situations described above may all be the handiwork of just one person, whose lack of boundaries shows up in various ways.

Logical consequences are the route to follow in dealing with this problem. You need to make clear rules and clear consequences regarding possessions, space, and privacy. You must be specific:

> "When the door to my room is closed, you must knock and wait for an answer before entering, and no means no. Don't come in."

> "You may not wear, borrow, or use anyone else's things without asking first. This includes pencils."

> "When you borrow something, you must return it."

Then create logical consequences for these rules, as in the following Suggestion Box.

Some Possible Consequences for Boundary Violations

1. Territory violations: Child can't leave his or her room for a specified time.

2. Taking others' possessions without permission: Child pays rent.

3. Not returning borrowed items: Child pays rent.

4. Losing another's possession: Child buys a new one.

When Shannon's parents explained the rules to her, she was amenable. Two days later as she was leaving for school, her younger sister, Ellen, came running down the stairs.

"Dad, Shannon is wearing my scarf. GIVE ME MY SCARF, SHANNON," she yelled.
"Don't be a cry baby, Ellen. It's only a scarf, " replied Shannon.

Should parents intervene in such an argument between the two siblings? The answer is an unqualified yes. Even if the argument is between the siblings, the parents are involved if the child has broken a family rule, in this case, the rule about borrowing possessions without asking.

"Did you ask Ellen if you could borrow her scarf?"
"No."
"Then please take it off and give it back to Ellen. You will have to pay Ellen rent on her scarf for taking it without asking, because that is the consequence we agreed on for borrowing things without permission. Remember the minimum rental time is one hour." (This meant that Shannon owed Ellen a dollar.)

There were many such encounters regarding issues of Shannon invading her siblings' and parents' space and privacy, taking others' possessions without permission, and not returning borrowed items. Each time there was a consequence. Slowly, ever so slowly, Shannon learned to be more aware of and more respectful of others' boundaries.

Be sure you do not have any boundary violators in your household. If you do, intervene early so that it does not turn into a major problem.

In regard to all the behaviors in this section, remember to "acknowledge the bits." Reward positive changes, even small ones.

CHAPTER THIRTEEN

Television and Telephones: Childhood's Inalienable Rights?

*T*elevision and telephones are the most cherished activities of childhood, ones that children and teenagers in our culture regularly enjoy. They actually are privileges that we adults allow them to have. But wait. This is only an adult's viewpoint. Most kids look at it a little differently. Television and telephones are part of childhood's bill of rights. From their perspective, it is not something that we grant them, but an inalienable right. To deny them one of these activities for any reason is tantamount to taking away their citizenship. It's cause for a full-scale rebellion. "Give me liberty and a TV."

The Use of Television and Telephones

Kids should not take these privileges for granted. Therefore, it is imperative to have well-thought-out and clear rules about these activities. The most important rules concern what, when, and how much.

If television and phones come with the territory of youth, kids don't have to earn these privileges, and they bring no particular responsibilities. As has been stressed throughout this book, however, children must be given responsibilities. Chores and certain duties, such as baby-sitting a younger sibling, fall into this category. Moreover, children need to learn that when they are allowed to have access to a television set, a phone, a stereo, or a computer, let alone to own one or more of these items, additional responsibilities come with these privileges.

TELEVISION: BLESSING OR CURSE?

Here is a common complaint by parents: "He watches TV all the time. I just can't get him to do other things."

The power of the visual image on a movie screen or a television screen is enormous. As we have all experienced, it can be hypnotic. There is quite a difference between television and the movies, however. You can't get hypnotized or "addicted" to the movies as easily as you can to TV for an obvious reason. Television is readily accessible. With a mere flick of the switch any time of the day or night, you can find something to watch. If children are allowed to watch TV whenever they want, it won't be long before they are hooked.

In addition, if kids spend too much time watching TV, they won't spend time exploring, playing make-believe, inventing, asking questions, and wondering. Why should a child wonder when he is watching cartoons? No imagination is needed there. Too much TV deadens the imagination. Put limits on the amount of time your children can watch TV.

Next, you must ask yourself *what* you want your children to see, realizing that, while they are watching, they are learning, especially the younger ones. Don't forget how powerful the visual image is. These shows provide powerful models for your children. They show them how to be. Recall what was discussed about modeling in Chapters Four and Five. Be sure you know what they are watching.

When my children were young, they loved to watch reruns of the "I Love Lucy" show every night. Belatedly, I watched some of these shows with them. After a while, I became quite concerned with what I saw. While these characters were basically harmless and, of course, quite funny, I did not like the role models for marital relationships that they were portraying. Many episodes, for instance, were based on trickery and deceit. So after a while, I did not allow them to watch the show. I wasn't too popular around the house for some time.

This show is nothing compared with what is on television today. There is a great deal of mindless material, as well as a considerable amount of violence and sex. If a child watches violence constantly, it is easy to become accustomed to and develop a callous to violence. And what about seeing women so often portrayed as sex objects, such as on MTV? Do you want young girls to believe that this is the way to act when they grow up? On the other hand, limited though it is, there is some very good programming. Help your children find it and encourage them to watch interesting subjects that they can learn from.

What do you do if your child wants to watch television constantly? Use the basic approach that I have been encouraging you to use. First, set a limit. Define exactly how much TV they can watch each day. Since TV is a privilege, use it as a reward. When they follow the rules, reward them occasionally with an extra show. On the other hand, if they go over the agreed upon time limit, withdraw the privilege. For example, if you discover that your child has watched for an extra half-hour, simply allow a half-hour less the following day (same idea as time banks).

If you find them watching shows that you have forbidden, ones that have violence, for example, use the same principle. Simply remove the privilege for a period of time. One father I know of put the TV in the garage for a week.

A word of caution: Don't use the watching of television as an all-purpose consequence for your kids: "You're late. No TV tonight." "You hit your sister, so you can't watch TV for two days." It is easy to fall into this rut. After a while, however, this consequence can lose its punch, and the kids will resent it. As I have been suggesting all along, tailor the consequences to the situation.

Also, don't use TV as a distraction for younger children. "Quit bothering me. Go watch TV for a while." Television becomes your baby-sitter in this case. There are better ways to occupy young children's time.

WORKING THE PHONES

When I was just starting out in psychology, I wanted to know everything I could about children. So I set off on a long journey to find a wise, old psychologist who could reveal the secrets of childrearing to me. After a long and arduous trek, I found him sitting on a golden pillow in the bell tower of a famous university. Falling to my knees, I implored him to reveal his wisdom to me. Beaming at me with a radiant smile, he said: "You must remember one thing about children, my son. The older they get, the more time they spend on the phone."

His prophetic words still ring true today. As kids grow older, they begin a long and dependent love affair with the telephone. And as teenagers, they are prone to treat the family phone as their own personal possession. Problems arise when they spend inordinate amounts of time on the phone so that it interferes with doing their chores and homework, not to mention that no one else in the family can use it. Sometimes parents also encounter problems with late-night calls, incoming as well as outgoing.

While the phone is commonplace and everyone takes it for granted, it should remain a privilege for kids. Have clear rules about phone usage, particularly during evenings. If your child's use of the phone becomes a problem, then specify how many calls may be made and received in the course of an evening, the maximum length of any given call, and at what time all calls must come to an end.

The consequence for failure to keep any of these agreements is simple. They must give up their phone privilege for some specified time period. There is no need for arguments, debates, and hassles over the phone. When they abuse their phone privilege, they simply can't use it. This consequence is powerful because whenever a teen or preteen can't use the phone, their life basically comes to an end.

This consequence should apply to incoming calls as well. Sometimes their friends may call at a late hour. "I can't help it," they'll say. Make clear to your kids that they are responsible when their friends call after the cutoff time. If they lose their phone privilege because of this late night activity, they'll soon tell their friends to stop calling late.

Should Kids Have Their Own Separate Phone Number?

It's 11:45 P.M. and the phone is ringing. You have been asleep all of twenty minutes, and in your dazed state you reach over and pick up the receiver by your nightstand, but get a dial tone. Yet, the phone is still ringing somewhere, and then it stops. It finally dawns on you. It's the other line, the one in your twelve-year-old's room.

The other guideline the old psychologist gave me was: "My son, never put a phone extension in a child's room." More and more these days even preteens want their own phone. Owning their own phone should be regarded with almost the same responsibility that comes with having a car. After all, phones cost money. Who is going to pay for the phone, the new line, and the monthly charge?

If you want to give your child her very own phone and separate line as a gift for her birthday, that's fine (in spite of the advice of the wise, old psychologist). But she should shoulder some of the responsibility, such as paying the monthly bill. When children have to pay their own phone bill, they have an excellent opportunity to learn about money and learn how privileges and responsibilities go hand in hand. They may even have to get a job to support their phone habit!

Furthermore, having their own phone does not give them complete autonomy about its use. There are still chores and homework to do and some sleep to be had. The same rules and agreements about the family phone should apply to their own phone. When you hear a phone ringing at 1:00 A.M., don't ignore it. A ring is a signal to answer the phone. A phone ringing at nearly midnight is another kind of signal for you—a signal to set a limit.

CONCLUSION:
LOOK AHEAD AND PREPARE NOW

The strategies provided in this section of the book not only enable you to help your child behave appropriately and to talk and relate to you effectively, they enable your child to be a responsible person given his or her age. Ultimately, this means being a good citizen.

As children grow older, they naturally want more freedom and privileges. They want to roam farther from home by themselves, they want to stay away longer, and they want to come and go at their own discretion. They want you around less and less, and they want to make their own choices about what they do and who they spend time with. Basically, they are moving more and more out of your direct control.

How can you be sure, then, that they will handle themselves well, even honorably? Of course there is no way to be absolutely sure, but if you have raised a responsible child, that child will become a responsible preteen, a responsible teen, and a responsible adult.

Consider driving. Would you like to know what just about the scariest moment in your whole life will be? It's the night your child takes the car out by herself for the first time.

After all these years, I still vividly remember seeing my mother standing at the window as I drove in that first night.

Do not let your child drive or much less own a car, unless you are completely sure that he or she is a responsible person. People who are responsible are mature and have good judgment. Contrary to what we would like to believe, these qualities do not miraculously appear on the sixteenth birthday. Teens think, "I'm sixteen. Now I can drive." Of course they can legally, and society has to have some way of establishing a standard, which age roughly provides.

As a parent you need to go further. You need to ask yourself whether your child is responsible enough to handle a car. Then you need to make an appropriate decision.

Moreover, you cannot suddenly and magically teach your child to be responsible at sixteen. At this age, it is a huge endeavor. Be sure, therefore, that long before sixteen comes along, your teenager is already responsible in his or her life. She follows rules, takes care of possessions, is responsible in using the phone, contributes to the family by doing chores, and so on. If she is responsible in these ways, she will be ready to take on the responsibility of driving a car.

Therefore, *now* is the time to train your children, not when they are twelve, or fourteen or sixteen. To wait is to court disaster. If they are not responsible, they will give you various signals, many of which have been dealt with in this section of the book. If they are responsible, you will surely know it, because there will be no signals.

CHAPTER FOURTEEN

Pervasive and Persistent Misbehavior: Correcting the Child You Can't Correct

You find yourself frustrated. You have tried everything you know, and you still cannot get your child to comply. This is the child who can't be corrected, the child who is disobedient and uncooperative in not just one or two ways as we have been discussing, but in ways too numerous to list. This is the child who is basically out of your control. Is it possible to gain control over such a child? Yes, it is; but first, consider the reason a child may be this way.

One reason can be that the child has attention deficit disorder. Children with this disorder, who are restless and inattentive and have a hard time following directions, are at a definite disadvantage in life and need special help. If you believe your child may possibly have this disorder, do not hesitate to ask for help. Probably the easiest and best place to start is through your school, which should be able to provide you with appropriate resources in your community that deal with this problem.

The second reason can be that the child has emotional problems. These problems may be the child's, or, as is often the case, they may reflect emotional problems within the family. In either case, it is extremely important for parents to consider this possibility and be willing to deal with it. Again, there are good resources in most communities for obtaining help for emotional problems.

This chapter deals with pervasive and persistent misbehavior that is due to poor training and bad habits. These problems can be corrected, although it takes a considerable amount of patience and determination.

You now have all the tools you need to discipline your kids effectively. These tools include having an effective parenting style; being sure that your child relates to you appropriately; setting clear limits; and using rewards, modeling, and natural and logical consequences to keep the limits in place. If you have been using them, minor discipline problems are probably clearing up. The challenge now is to use these tools to deal with more difficult discipline problems. There is really nothing new in this chapter, except that it will show you how to use these tools systematically to deal with the hard-to-manage child.

INDICATORS OF DIFFICULT DISCIPLINE PROBLEMS

Here is a list of some of the difficult misbehaviors that parents encounter. Look at them as signals your child is sending to you. Something is wrong and needs fixing. Do not ignore them!

Lying	Not doing chores
Running away	Having uncontrolled rages
Disrupting the class	Fighting incessantly with
Stealing	siblings
Cutting classes	Destroying property
Hitting parents	Bullying
Having frequent and	Hitting other children
multiple misbehaviors	

Typically, problems start off in little ways; but then one minor problem leads to another and then another, until at some point, parents find themselves facing numerous roadblocks in disciplining one or more of their children. Feelings of being overwhelmed soon follow, as the parents and their kids engage in what seem like endless power struggles. These struggles go on and on with the same issues recycling, and it becomes quite difficult to find a way out. At this point, parents often feel trapped and helpless. While there are many variations, these cycles go something like this:

Child misbehaves—parent punishes—child emotionally reacts to the punishment—parent reacts emotionally to the child's reaction—child resists—cycle starts over again—child misbehaves—parent punishes—child reacts—parent packs his or her bags

At some point, it all usually simmers down, and a brief respite ensues, without any real solution. You can bet your bags the cycle will soon return.

The Key to Handling Difficult Misbehavior

You can easily be overwhelmed and confused when encountering persistent and pervasive misbehavior. The key is to break it down into smaller parts. First, deal with oppositional styles, and then with one misbehavior at a time.

REASONS FOR MISBEHAVIOR

There are three possible reasons that kids misbehave: A parent's style is not effective, the child's style is interfering with discipline, and/or the misbehavior is not being handled correctly. One or all of these may be the cause of persistent and pervasive misbehavior. Therefore, you need to be aware of these possibilities and set the following goals, to be carried out sequentially:

1. **Be sure your parenting style is effective.**
2. **Be sure your child's style is appropriate (not oppositional).**
3. **Have effective strategies for handling misbehavior.**

RELATING COMES FIRST

Persistent discipline problems always involve difficulties in relating and getting along. Never-ending power struggles are invariably accompanied by upset and unhappiness in the parent-child relationship. And sometimes it goes the other way. Parents and kids have difficulties in getting along, and kids react by resisting their parents and becoming harder to manage. The following Suggestion Box is not a new idea to you at this point; but when parents are dealing with a hard-to-manage child, it is absolutely critical to follow this recommendation.

Relating and Discipline

Whatever the reason for discipline problems, no matter which is the chicken and which is the egg, you always want to be sure you and your child are relating effectively first.

Check Your Parenting Style

Before you attempt any changes, examine your parenting style. Watch yourself as you interact with your children around discipline. Perhaps you have a pleasing style, so that you end up being too lenient and your kids don't have sufficient limits. Perhaps you are too bossy and controlling, and the kids, feeling squeezed, are reacting to that.

If necessary, review Chapter One to refresh your understanding and awareness of styles. Then watch yourself as you go about disciplining your children. If you are unclear about your style, you can ask others for feedback. Also notice any situations that push your buttons. With this awareness, you can substitute the firm, gentle style for the one you have been using as you apply the techniques in this chapter. (Remember that it takes practice, and you don't have to be perfect.)

Take your time with this. Don't try to change your child's behavior until you are sure that your parenting style is effective. Otherwise, you will undermine your efforts. Starting with yourself is a prudent and usually fruitful decision.

THE GAME PLAN FOR PERSISTENT MISBEHAVIOR

Once you have checked out your parenting style and have made whatever changes you think are necessary, you are ready to address your child's behavior. As mentioned earlier, the key to dealing with persistent and pervasive misbehavior is to break it down into smaller, more manageable pieces. You won't be surprised at this point to see that the game plan for changing your child's behavior has two parts, one dealing with oppositional styles and one dealing with misbehavior.

The Overall Strategy For Changing Persistent Misbehavior

Change your child's oppositional style:

1. Observe your child's style.
2. Sort out the styles and target the least emotionally intense one for change.
3. Use modeling and rewards to change the style.
4. Use logical consequences if the style persists.
5. Repeat steps three and four to deal with any other oppositional style.

Address misbehavior:

1. Identify any remaining problem behaviors.
2. Select a specific misbehavior to change.
3. Use natural and logical consequences for misbehavior, and acknowledge and reward the desired behavior.
4. Repeat steps three and four with any other misbehaviors.

These strategies are discussed in detail throughout the book and the examples that follow show you how to put them together in a systematic way to change difficult and entrenched patterns of misbehavior. Each point in the strategy is explained as it is applied to the detailed examples that illustrate how a child's difficult and persistent misbehavior was successfully changed.

When there are ongoing discipline problems, there is usually a buildup of tension in the family. It is desirable, then, to create a positive context in which to make the changes. Moreover, all changes, even positive ones, are somewhat disruptive. First, break down whatever barriers that may have arisen in your relationship because of the ongoing conflicts and create some positive momentum. The following Suggestion Box offers some guidelines.

Approach Your Kids Before Making Changes

First, talk to your children about how you see the situation. Kids like to know what is going on. They want to know what you think and how you see things. This will help them to feel included. Explain the problems to them without blaming or shaming.

Briefly lay out the problems as you see them, and then get their opinions about them. Give them a chance to express themselves. Listen to their input. Sometimes parents are amazed at the observations that kids can

continued

make. One parent reported that her daughter thought the problems were due to Mom telling her one thing and Dad another, and she recommended that her parents talk things over and try to do things the same way.

Next, own your side of the problem. We like to think we are faultless, but few of us are (this is particularly embarrassing when you are a psychologist). We all make mistakes. If we take an honest approach with our kids and admit our deficiencies, it makes it easier for our kids to do the same.

You might say, "I know I have been yelling at you a lot lately, and I'm sorry. I am going to stop doing this. I know it makes you feel bad, and I don't feel very good about it." Or say, "I've been too critical of you, and I am going to make every effort to change that."

Then go on to tell them what you would like them to change. Be very specific and give examples: "Remember what happened yesterday when I asked you to bring in the toys from the backyard and you argued with me? You've been arguing with me a lot lately, and that's not okay."

Ask them for their reaction and whether they want help with the problem. Let them know that you want to work together so that things can go well between you. "You'll try not to argue, and I'll try very hard not to yell and raise my voice."

Rather than trying to solve problems, it is important at this point to create a positive context and agree upon goals. If your child doesn't agree or doesn't think there are any problems, don't try to convince him or her that here are. That will only make the child defensive. Just let it go, and use the methods in this chapter.

Some Guidelines for Applying the Strategies

1. **Start with issues that are directly between you and your child.** When kids are hard to manage, they often have behavioral problems in other settings outside the home, for example, school, Cub Scouts and Brownies, and sports activities. This is often a signal to parents that the problems are more serious than they realized. Although the problems in other settings must eventually be addressed, they are not the place to begin. Start with the problems that are right in front of you; those that you can deal with directly.

2. **Be persistent and consistent.** Because persistent misbehavior and oppositional styles of relating are automatic and entrenched, they are not going to disappear the first time you address them. It will take consistent use of the methods in this chapter. And it will take persistence, as you encounter resistance and even escalation of the problems initially. Don't stop when you encounter resistance. If you keep applying the methods, you will be successful.

3. **Talk to your children as you go along.** Find out what they are feeling about the changes that you and they are making. Find out what is hard for them and what suggestions they have.

4. **Work on one problem at a time.** Don't try to change all the problems at once, whether you are concerned with a style or a misbehavior. Working on one issue at a time allows you to focus and concentrate. It is just plain easier. When you have succeeded with one problem, move on to the next. This creates positive momentum.

5. **Be constantly on the lookout for how you may be rewarding the very styles and behaviors that you don't want.** While rewards come in many guises, the most important ones are your time and attention,

which can be particularly powerful in keeping oppositional styles going. As you now know, paying attention to and responding to your child when she is
arguing rewards the arguing. Therefore, you must be
sure that you are not rewarding misbehavior, even as
you are going about trying to change it.

Don't give up if changes don't occur right away. After all, the
misbehavior didn't appear overnight. Just pay attention to
what goes on in your interaction and plug away at it, using the
strategies that are in this chapter.

Now let's proceed with the game plan.

THE BENEFITS OF OBSERVING

Before launching into action, you must take some time to
observe your child's style. Although mentioned previously, I
want to explain observing in more detail. There are three reasons for doing careful observations. First, you will be able to
identify the various aspects of the style more clearly. When kids
persistently misbehave, they invariably have developed an array
of ways to resist and oppose you. Sorting these out through
observation will enable you to be clear about where to start.

Second, you will be able to identify some of the situations
that trigger oppositional styles and will be able to anticipate
these situations so that you are not caught off guard. For
example, if your child complains every night when it is time
to go to bed, then you can be ready for it and have a plan to
deal with the complaining.

Third, you can discover how and if you are rewarding a style
that you don't want. You might, for instance, discover that
when your child whines, he gets a lot of attention, or that
when he screams at you, you give in.

Observing need not be difficult or complicated. But you
will need to take a few days to do it so that you can get some
good examples of problematic styles.

Keep some paper and pencil handy, and when a negative style occurs, write down exactly what happens. Record the dialogue, along with the emotional tones in the conversation, as specifically as you can. Pretend that you are writing a script for a movie or television scene. That is how graphically clear it should be. Be sure to include your own responses and as much of the interaction as you can, and try to do this right after it happens so that your memory is fresh.

Get as many examples as you can over a few days. After you have some typical examples, then you can keep a count as the familiar reactions occur. Parents are often amazed at how revealing this exercise is. They discover aspects of their child's style that they weren't noticing: "I didn't know she nagged me so much." Or, "I knew he argued with me a lot, but I had no idea how demanding he is." Often parents see very clearly how they are giving attention to and therefore rewarding resistive behavior. Some actual parental observations are given in the following examples.

STEPHEN, AGE EIGHT

Joan and Barry enrolled in a parenting class that I was teaching. They had three major concerns about their son Stephen. First, they said that he didn't like school and a couple of times a month refused to go. Moreover, he wasn't applying himself and was not doing his homework on a regular basis. Second, he became easily frustrated, his responses quickly escalating into yelling and screaming. And third, he often refused to comply with their directions and requests. He did his chores irregularly at best and frequently disobeyed their rules, most notably by not coming home on time and by going out of the neighborhood without permission. Joan and Barry were worn down and desperate.

Following the guidelines, they decided to deal with the issues in the home first, even though they were primarily concerned with his school-related problems. Their first task was to be sure that the relating in the home went well. This meant that they had to check and evaluate their own and Stephen's style of relating.

Joan and Barry's Parenting Styles

Before attempting to make any changes with Stephen, they examined their styles of parenting. Although their individual styles were quite similar, they realized that there were some problems. Over the years, they had tried too hard to please their son, and as his behavior had become more and more difficult to handle, they had resorted to spankings and threatening him with punishment when he didn't do what they asked. This mixture of pleasing him on the one hand and threats and spanking on the other was confusing to Stephen. They soon realized that their ways of handling him were not working.

Once they saw these parenting styles more clearly, they felt that they could change to a firmer, gentler style. Then they were ready to start the process of changing Stephen's behavior.

Observations

Joan and Barry spent a week observing Stephen, to get a closer look at and an understanding of his style. They both made observations, although, since Joan was at home, she made most of them. She took the time to make careful and detailed notes, and here are some of them, exactly as she wrote them down:

Friday Morning

Stephen got up early and came into my room at 6:30 half dressed. Before I could say anything, he grumpily complained that his alarm had gone off early and then he left. When I came downstairs, he said, "I'm not putting on my shoes and socks because I'm not going to school."

A while later I told him to put his shoes and socks on so that his feet wouldn't get cold. "All right, but I'm not going to school."

I asked him about his lunch and he crossly replied, "I don't care. I'm not going to school."

Still later, he said he wasn't going to school. I said calmly, "Yes, you are." He stomped upstairs, shouting, "I'm not going and you can't make me."

I told him that his father would come home later that morning after a meeting to see that he got to school. He screamed, "He can't make me go either."

Saturday Morning

After breakfast and watching TV, I told Stephen it was time to get his Saturday chores done.

He replied crossly, "What do I have to do now?"

I said, "You know what your Saturday job is—raking the lawn and sweeping the basement."

Stephen said, "I want to go outside and play. I don't want to do it."

I said, "Oh, yes, come on, let's get started."

"I want to go out and play. You said I could yesterday."

"I said that you could play after you did your chores."

"Well, I'm not going downstairs to get the things I need."

About two minutes later, he went down for the cleaning things and did a hasty job.

Later Joan noted that this type of exchange occurred at least two or three times a day in response to agreed upon chores or other small requests she would make of him, such as filling the dog's dish with water.

Sunday

I asked, "Did you brush your teeth after breakfast?"

Stephen made a sour face and said, "No."

I said, "You need to do that at least twice a day." He sat on the stairs and said, "I'm not going upstairs just to brush my teeth and that's that."

"Stephen," I called, "Come up here please."

"What for?" he replied.

"I want you to get your teeth brushed before you go out."

"I'm not going up just to brush my teeth," he yelled.

I said, "I'm sure I can find you something else to do up here."

He went outside without brushing his teeth.

Later That Day

At lunch time, I asked Stephen if he wanted some lunch. He said he had eaten at a friend's. I asked what he had and he said, "Toast." Then he headed for the refrigerator to get some donuts we had for dessert. I said I felt he needed something else for lunch besides toast. He clenched his fists and screamed at me, "I don't want anything else!" With that he left the kitchen and slammed the door. A minute later, I went into the family room and asked if he would like me to fix him soup. He said no. Then I suggested I fry him an egg. His reply was, "Fix me a big glass of orange juice, too." I said I would be happy to if he said please. He said, "Please," but raised his voice.

When she reviewed her notes on this particular observation, Joan realized that she had fallen back into her pleasing style. Falling back is bound to happen, because styles are such ingrained habits. The more we become aware of them, however, the less automatic they become. Here is one of Barry's observations:

Sunday Afternoon

Stephen was just finishing playing Monopoly with a friend who had won. Stephen was throwing the money and cards into the box when I told him I wanted him to stack it properly. He said to me, "I'm not going to put it away like that. I didn't find it all stacked up." I told him to do it anyway so that things wouldn't get lost. He shouted, "No." In a soft voice I said, "I won't let you have friends stay overnight if you are going to act like this." He began to pick up the cards, and his friend began to take care of the paper money.

In this situation, Barry realized that even though he had used a soft voice, he had nonetheless used a threat to motivate Stephen.

From these and other observations, Stephen's parents could see that while Stephen easily and quickly had tantrums, his argumentativeness occurred much more often. A rough count of these behaviors showed that while Stephen yelled and screamed at them about eight times during the six days of observing, he argued with them about twenty times. Joan and Barry could see very clearly why they were worn out by Stephen's style and why they were feeling angry with him. Their first intervention was to deal with his argumentative way of relating, a level-two style.

Changing Stephen's Style

Sitting down together to discuss how they were going to proceed, Joan and Barry realized that the first step was to stop rewarding him for his arguing. Their listening to him, their reasoning with him, and even their arguing with him all provided interpersonal rewards for the behavior they did not like or want.

They decided that they would not interact with him when he argued and would use a logical consequence when he would not stop. They decided to promote a more respectful style by modeling it for him and rewarding it with their attention and affection.

First, they sat him down and explained the problem to him. They told him that they noticed that he argued with them a lot and that this was no longer acceptable. When they asked him how he felt about all the arguments and disagreements they were having, he said he was unhappy about it. They agreed that they were, too. They said that they would no longer spank him or threaten him, but that he needed to try to stop arguing. Nothing was said at this point about his yelling and screaming.

Then they modeled for him how they wanted him to talk to them and invited him to try it. After some initial balking, Stephen reluctantly tried out what his parents suggested, and they told him that they really appreciated his efforts.

The next couple of weeks were not easy. Their most difficult challenge was to stay focused on his argumentative style and not respond to the yelling and screaming. If the latter got too overwhelming, they would send him to his room. Whenever Stephen argued and talked defiantly, they would immediately point it out to him and ask him to try it again, gently reminding him of their talk. At first he refused to try, so they had to introduce a logical consequence: "You can either make an attempt to talk in a respectful way or you will have to stay inside this afternoon. It is up to you."

The first three times he stayed in. But they did not pressure him, get angry, or make him wrong. They just gave him the choice. They ignored several tantrums that followed his having to stay inside and reminded him that it was up to him. Finally, Stephen began to realize that arguing wasn't getting him what he wanted; he made some attempts to modify his style, correcting himself or asking if he could repeat what he had said in a more acceptable way. Immediately, his parents acknowledged him for this, telling him how much they appreciated his trying.

Joan and Barry were surprised and pleased to notice that after this had happened a few times, the tension between Stephen and them began to lessen. They didn't feel at odds with him as much, and he seemed less angry.

As the tension in the house started to dissolve, Stephen received frequent acknowledgement for talking and relating in respectful and appropriate ways, as his parents took pains to let him know how much they appreciated the way he was talking to them. One night they took the family out for pizza (Stephen's favorite food) because he had been making such a strong effort.

After about two weeks, Barry and Joan realized that Stephen's argumentativeness had reduced by eighty percent. Moreover, they were no longer hearing his hallmark phrase: "You can't make me." Barry and Joan were hopeful that a positive cycle was being established.

They next decided to tackle his yelling and screaming, which they noticed had already decreased somewhat. Whenever it occurred, however, it had a big impact on the family. They added a little wrinkle to their approach. Since it is difficult to talk to someone who is yelling, they set up a signal with him. Whenever he raised his voice or started to yell, they raised their right hand in the air. This was his signal to stop. If he did, they acknowledged him for it and gave him another chance to talk in a calm way. If he did not stop, the same consequence they had used previously went into effect automatically, which was that he had to stay in for the rest of the day or the next day if it occurred in the evening.

Because Stephen had gained some self-control by learning to contain his argumentativeness, he was able to respond to the signal most of the time. Within a week, his yelling and screaming had diminished considerably. At this point, the arguing had almost completely disappeared and little remained of his once formidable oppositional style.

Within about four weeks, including the observation period, Barry and Joan had made it possible for Stephen to develop an appropriate style of responding and relating to them. This was no small accomplishment, considering how strongly entrenched Stephen's oppositional style had been. Both Stephen and his parents had every right to feel good about what they had accomplished.

Correcting Stephen's Misbehavior

Once Stephen's style had become acceptable, Joan and Barry could then address his misbehavior. While they had been primarily concerned about his school problems, they now realized that they had many problems with him in their home besides his arguing and yelling. He did few of his chores and generally did not follow their rules, particularly about where he could go in the neighborhood and about being home on time.

They were now pleasantly surprised to discover that he seemed generally more compliant. He was not resisting nearly as much the simple requests they made of him, such as to take out the garbage or to bring his toys in from outside. This improved cooperation is usually the case. When a child is no longer reacting with a negative and oppositional style, his behavior improves. Although improved, he was still not doing his chores on a regular basis and still was frequently late.

Barry and Joan then addressed these issues separately with him. First, they tackled the lateness problem, using the strategies in the section on Late Times and Bedtimes. They set up a time-bank program for him. Although he balked somewhat initially, since he no longer was so automatically oppositional, he soon was coming home on time.

Next, they set clear rules and consequences for him concerning his chores, following the strategies in the section on Chores and Homework. They realized that although they had clearly stated the chores for Stephen, they had not set up consequences. Since Stephen loved to be out playing with his friends, they simply used this as the consequence. When he finished his chores, he was allowed to go out and even earned extra time with his friends. When he failed to do a chore, he lost time with his friends. Joan and Barry were happy to find that this worked well, and soon Stephen was cooperating. ˙

Finally, they tackled his homework problem. His attitude was already beginning to change, and they noticed he was no longer defiantly stating that he wasn't going to go to school. However, he still was not doing his homework on a regular basis.

Joan and Barry set up a plan with Stephen's teacher. He was to write down his homework every day and have his teacher initial it. He now had to complete his homework after school, before he could go out to play. When he finished his homework, he could go out until dinnertime. When he had successfully completed his homework three days in a row, he could begin doing his homework after dinner. If at any time he did not finish his homework in the evening, the plan would begin over again; and he would have to do his homework after school once again for another three-day cycle, until he would be allowed to do it after dinner.

Joan and Barry made it very clear to Stephen that the choice was his. They did not nag him or argue with him about it. When they discussed this with him, Stephen immediately reverted to his old form and began arguing. They listened for about twenty seconds and then interrupted him to remind him that he was raising his voice; they suggested that he voice his objections more appropriately. Stephen paused and then in a fairly calm voice told his parents that he did not think it was fair.

> "I understand that you don't think this is fair, Stephen," said Joan. "But you are not doing your homework regularly and you must learn to do that. Do you have a better way that would get you to do it?"
>
> "I promise I'll do it right after dinner from now on," the rather desperate boy replied.
>
> "I know you mean it Stephen," his Dad said. "But you've gotten into some bad habits, and your mom and I think this is a better way. The promise doesn't guarantee that you'll do it. Our plan is better. I appreciate your stating it calmly and not raising your voice."

Stephen understood the plan, and because there was now a cooperative spirit between him and his parents, the plan went smoothly. He did his homework for the three days in a row after school and then was allowed to do it after dinner. He slipped once a few days later and had to do it after school again for three days. After that there were no more hitches, and his homework was done regularly.

In a little less than seven weeks, Stephen's behavior and style of relating had changed markedly. He had become respectful of his parents and was complying with what they expected of him. This was accomplished by following the program carefully and consistently, taking it step-by-step, and not rushing through it.

The keys were not rewarding his oppositional style, not letting it pay off in any way, and providing interpersonal rewards for an appropriate way of relating. This turned around the tension and discomfort between Stephen and his parents, and made it possible to resolve other problems quickly.

Here is a summary of the main elements in the program for Stephen:

Main concerns:

1. Not doing school work
2. Yelling and screaming
3. Noncompliance with chores and rules

Strategies:

1. Change parental styles from pleasing and threatening to gentle, firm style
2. Target arguing
   - Remove rewards (listening and arguing back)
   - Model and reward desired style
   - Set up logical consequences for undesirable style
3. Target yelling and screaming
   - Signal to stop
   - Set up logical consequence for screaming
   - Encourage, acknowledge, and reward desired style
4. Target noncompliance in home
   - Set up program for habitual lateness, using time banks
   - Set up clear consequences for not doing chores

5. Target resistance to doing homework
   - Enlist teacher cooperation
   - Set up logical consequence: do homework right after school
   - Add reward: do homework after dinner

KRISTIN, AGE 5

Rosemary was a teacher and a single parent who consulted me about her daughter Kristin, who was in kindergarten. Her main concern was that Kristin was "too aggressive" with children both in the neighborhood and at school. She would push, trip, and hit other kids. Recently, at a friend's home, she had deliberately knocked a glass of juice out of a girl's hand. The final straw was that at school she had swung a stick and hit another child with it.

At home Kristin balked at doing her chores, such as feeding the dog, setting the table, and tidying her room. She was also demanding and bossy toward her mother.

Rosemary's Parenting Style

When I asked Rosemary about how she handled Kristin, she was quite candid about her parenting style:

> "From the beginning I've been too critical. I know it was the way I was raised. I could never do anything right, and now I'm afraid that I'm taking the same approach with Kristin. Now that things are out of hand, I don't know what to do and I get mad and yell at her (enforcer style). I yell too much, but I don't know what else to do anymore."

Rosemary was very upset and went on to say tearfully, "I don't know how to change things." She was clearly blaming herself and feeling enormously guilty. I told Rosemary that many, if not most, parents automatically parent the way they were brought up, that this was often an ineffective model, and that usually parents have problems training their children not because they are incompetent but because they don't have the needed tools.

I explained to her the firm, gentle style of parenting. With some concentration, determination, and practice, Rosemary worked on her parenting style and was able to change it.

Observations

Next, she spent a few days observing Kristin's style. While she knew that Kristin was bossy and demanding, she was surprised to discover how frequently Kristin whined, complained, and nagged. These behaviors occurred several times a day. Here are a couple of brief excerpts from her notes:

Monday Evening

> "It's time to set the table, Kristin."
> "Do I have to?" (spoken in a high-pitched, nasal tone)
> "Yes, you have to."
> "I always have to do all the work." (same tone)
> "Kristin, set the table now."
> "Mom, you always make me set the table." She continued grumbling under her breath.
> A minute later: "Why do I always have to set the table?" (whining tone)

Saturday Morning

> "Mom, can I go over to Shannon's?"
> "After you have finished picking up your room."
> Two minutes later: "Can I go to Shannon's now?"
> "Did you finish your chores?"
> "No." (in a loud, exasperated voice)
> Five minutes later: "When can I go to Shannon's?"
> "When you finish your chores." (angrily)

Rosemary found that these exchanges affected her more than she realized. They were particularly draining after a day of teaching. It was clear that the whining, complaining, and nagging, mostly level-one behavior, was the place to start in changing Kristin's style.

The aggressive behavior could not be completely ignored, however. Rosemary set up clear, agreed upon consequences that would come into play whenever she hit another child or was aggressive in any way. I also encouraged her to talk to Kristin about what she was feeling when these events occurred.

Changing Kristin's Style

Following the guidelines and strategies outlined earlier in the chapter, Rosemary began by talking over the problems with Kristin and modeled for her the behavior she wanted, focusing only on the level-one behavior and, for the time being, ignoring the demanding, bossy part of her style, which was a mixture of levels two and three.

When Kristin complained, whined, or nagged, Rosemary simply pointed it out and asked her to try it again. At first, Kristin was frustrated with her mother; but Rosemary stood her ground and neither criticized Kristin nor raised her voice, simply saying, "You may not talk to me in that tone of voice. Try it again."

Begrudgingly, Kristin made some small efforts, which Rosemary immediately acknowledged her for, often giving her a hug and encouraging her. Rosemary reported that after a little over a week the atmosphere between mother and daughter was clearly changing. Rosemary was not criticizing her or yelling at her, and Kristin's nagging, complaining, and whining had dropped off markedly.

Rosemary then used the same procedure with her demanding and bossy behavior. In just a few days, this behavior reduced notably, following a few reminders from Rosemary. Now a positive cycle was being established between them that improved their relationship and reduced Kristin's resistance.

Chores became easier for Kristin to do. She was feeding the dog and setting the table. Tidying her room, however, was another matter. Rosemary made a rule that Kristin had to pick up her toys and clothes every evening; and she put in place a consequence—if she did not put her toys and clothes away, they would be put on a shelf in Mom's room for a week. Within a few days this problem was solved.

Kristin was now relating well to her mother and was cooperating. Rosemary, of course, was still quite concerned about her aggressive behavior. In the previous two weeks, she realized that she had had no reports of this behavior, nor had she observed any around her friends. At this point, our consultation ended.

I made a follow-up call to Rosemary four weeks later and learned that there had been only one incident in which Kristin had pushed another child at school and that it had been quickly resolved. Her aggressive behavior seemed to be gone. This is in line with what has been pointed out in previous chapters. When the relational problems around discipline clear up, many of the more difficult behavioral problems get better as well, without any further intervention.

Here is a summary of the program for Kristin:

Parental concerns:
1. Aggressive behavior
2. Balking at chores

Strategies:
1. Change parental style from critical and enforcing to firm, gentle style
2. Target complaining, whining, and nagging
3. Target demanding and bossy style
4. Target picking up toys and clothes

SUMMARY

A good relationship is hard to resist, and it is hard to resist when the relationship is good. When applied to the parent-child relationship, this means that when the relating is effective, the overall relationship will be good, and resistance on the part of the child will not go beyond what is expected at any given age. It is hard to be resistive, let alone oppositional, in a good relationship.

Thus, when it comes to managing your kids, make effective relating the priority. Be sure *that* is working first. Do this from the start and do it all along. If problems arise, take a close look at the way you are relating.

Kristin and Stephen had become difficult children to handle, and their resistance and misbehavior showed in different ways. But in both cases, changes needed to be made to the styles of relating. When these changes were made, the door was opened for discipline to go well.

Of course, children don't make these changes on their own. Parents must initiate the changes and help and guide them. When they do, parents can look forward to a happy household and years of enjoyment with their children.

CHAPTER FIFTEEN

Questions and Answers

Q: You haven't mentioned anything about timeouts. I use timeouts frequently with my children, but they don't seem to be effective. And sometimes they won't stay in their rooms until the timeout is over.

A: These days almost everyone knows about using timeouts, but not everyone knows how to use them correctly. A timeout often becomes a punishment. A child is misbehaving and the parent says, "You need a timeout. Go to your room." This is not a timeout; it is punishment.

The purpose of a timeout is to break a cycle, to prevent a situation from getting out of control or to allow the child to calm down. In basketball when an opposing team goes on a scoring run, the coach will call a timeout in order to put a break in the action and not let the game get out of control.

Timeouts can be useful for adults, too. Many marital therapists advise couples to take a break if they are getting too emotional or if they are arguing fruitlessly and can't resolve a particular issue. Taking breaks allows people to regroup.

The same is true when dealing with kids. Use timeouts mainly when kids are getting out of control, when they are so emotionally upset that it is pointless to try to correct them.

During a timeout, have your child go to a neutral place, *not her room*. I saw a great cartoon recently that showed a boy who had received a timeout, sitting on his bed in his room with his stereo and TV on, playing with his Game Boy, and using his own phone to order a pizza. Some timeout! Have your child sit in the dining room or in some quiet place in the house where he or she can be alone.

The timeout should be brief—for very young children, just a couple of minutes at most. It is not a punishment; it is a time to settle down. When your child is calm, then address the issue once again and apply the methods we have been using. And let's be honest, sometimes the timeout is for us, too, so that we also can regroup and stay calm. (If the timeout is really for you, then tell your child: "I need a timeout right now so I can think things over. We'll talk again in five minutes.")

What if your child won't comply with the timeout? Suppose that you give your five-year-old a timeout for three minutes and after a minute he leaves the timeout area. Simply escort him back to the timeout area and start the timeout over again, explaining this to him. You may have to do this several times at first. Stay calm and focus on having the timeout complied with so that you can once again address the problem that necessitated using it in the first place.

An older child may defy you by going to her room or even leaving the house. In this case, you need to do two things: Finish the timeout and add a consequence for leaving the timeout period without permission.

During an argument with his mom, Curtis started yelling and then ran off and slammed the door to his room. His mom then had him take a timeout; but before it was over, he went outside. She brought him back to finish the timeout and then discussed the situation with him, giving him a consequence for leaving the house in the middle of the timeout.

The purpose of a timeout is to restore some order so that you can deal with problems effectively. It is a strategy to help a child gain some self-control in a situation.

Q: I have been following your recommendations, but my child is getting worse, not better. He used to be argumentative and demanding. Now he is outright defiant. What should I do now?

A: This is not uncommon. Nine out of ten times the reason for this is what I refer to as upping the ante. It goes like this: A child sees that his parents are taking a new approach and that it has some zip. He realizes that his game is up, or is about to be. So, being the clever little fellow that he is, he ups the ante. He reacts with more gusto. In your case, instead of merely arguing, he starts being defiant, yelling and shouting when he can't have his way.

This point is quite crucial: If you back down by giving him what he wants or if you engage him, you will inadvertently reward this new, but worse, behavior. "This is working," he thinks. "Now I've got them where I want them again."

Just be sure you do not reward the new misbehavior. Use consequences for the misbehavior, and encourage and acknowledge the desired behavior.

You must be persistent. Changing these behavior patterns is not easy. Don't give up by giving in. Persistence pays off.

Q: I don't know what to do. It seems like there are so many things to deal with all at once. The other day I told my son Kevin to pick up his toys, which were strewn all around the house. Kevin wanted to go to the playground to meet a friend. When I said no, that he had to pick up his toys first, he began to argue. Again I said no. Then Kevin ran to his room and slammed the door. When I went to his room, he yelled at me and refused to come out. When I insisted he come out, he screamed at me and ran out of the house. I found him at the playground.

A: Situations like this not only try your patience but also can make your hair fall out. Everything hits at once. Misbehavior is followed by an oppositional style, followed by more misbehavior, more resistance, more misbehavior, more opposition, all in a matter of two or three minutes. It may seem like seconds. It is not just a storm cloud, it is a series of tornadoes.

These situations can be so overwhelming that the temptation is to let them go and either pretend they didn't happen or just give up and pray that it doesn't happen again. Well, don't give up. There are some things you can do.

When you run into a series of misbehaviors all at once, step back and look at what happened. Break down the situation. Problems, any kind of problems, are easier to handle when you break them into parts. When looked at closely, you'll find that there are four issues in Kevin's behavior.

1. Kevin argued.
2. He slammed his door.
3. He defied you by refusing to come out of his room.
4. He ran away from you and went to the playground.

You can't deal with all four of these misbehaviors at the same time, but you must deal with some of them. If you try to deal with all of them, you would just be loading Kevin up with consequences, which would seem like severe punishment to him and would not accomplish much, except to make him more resentful. If you give him one huge consequence for all the behaviors, he'd also be resentful. If you ignore his behavior, then you would be giving him permission to act that way.

Here is what to do: Sit down with him and talk over what happened. Ask to hear his side. Suppose that he tells you that it was really important to him to meet his friend because they were going to make a fort in the park next to the playground. You can say something like this:

"I understand that the fort was important to you, Kevin, From now on, please tell me the things that are important to you and then I can understand. But your behavior was not acceptable."

Then list the four problem behaviors for him. Give him consequences for two of them. For example, say, "For running away you have to stay in the house for the next two days after school. For arguing, you cannot have your friends over during this time or talk to them on the phone."

Tie the consequences as closely to his behavior as you can. The grounding is tied to his behavior of running out of the house without your permission. Because he argued, he can neither see his friends nor talk to them. And of course, he has to pick up his toys, the original issue.

Q: My four-year-old has temper tantrums, and one of his favorite places to have them is in the supermarket. How should I handle them?

A: There is no easy way to handle tantrums in public places, and you really can't correct them when you are out and about. You could try walking away from him, but you do not want to let him out of your sight or scare him by disappearing. Most parents are quite embarrassed by this behavior and would themselves like to disappear into thin air.

The best thing to do, if you can, is not to take him with you for a while and to work on the problem at home. By now you know that the tantrum is most likely not the only oppositional style you are running into. Therefore, assess the situation and start with his least emotionally intense style. Once he calms down at home, it's not likely that you will encounter tantrums in the supermarket.

Q: My daughter is cooperative at home and rarely disobeys, but at school and sometimes at Brownies she acts up and is disruptive. I don't understand why this is, and I have no idea what to do about it.

A: This is a difficult problem, and you may need some professional help to get the solution. But first, look closely at your parenting style. This problem sometimes occurs when a parent's style is too authoritarian. It may be too forceful or too bossy or intimidating in some way, making the child afraid to respond. But the anger may be inside her, and coming out in another setting.

Check out your style to see if you need to make any changes. If the problem remains after doing so, get a referral to a mental health professional.

PART FOUR

How Effective Discipline Increases a Child's Self-Control and Self-Esteem

*H*ow you discipline your child has effects beyond the immediate discipline situation. Because the disciplinary process goes on for many years, it has a huge impact on a child. We have already seen that it affects relationships. In this section, we will see how it affects a child's emotional system.

Discipline imposes external controls on a child, who does not have the ability to do this for herself. Over time she internalizes these controls and is then able to regulate her own behavior appropriately. Chapter Sixteen makes you aware of how you can directly help your child acquire this important trait.

The final chapter shows how discipline affects the way children feel about themselves—their self-esteem. When parents and children relate effectively, children feel accepted. When parents set limits appropriately, children feel increased security. Both of these factors make a significant contribution to the development of good self-esteem.

CHAPTER SIXTEEN

Fostering Self-Control

*O*ne way of viewing the hard-to-manage children described in the last section is that in addition to their behavior problems, they were lacking in self-control. When children have self-control problems, they have difficulty not only with accepting limits from others but also with placing limits on themselves.

Self-control is the ability to be in command of oneself. This means that a person is in control of their feelings, needs, and impulses. The ability of a child to contain himself or herself is critical to becoming a mature, responsible individual.

Self-control issues show up in a variety of ways. As already noted, children lacking in this trait are harder to discipline. They may also have difficulties in paying attention to social cues, in handling frustration, in waiting for what they want, and in listening to others. They tend to be demanding and have problems in initiating responsible behavior and guiding themselves.

Self-control issues manifest themselves in many different ways in day-to-day life: the three-year-old has daily temper tantrums; the four-year-old hits other children at nursery school; the five-year-old whines when other kids won't do exactly what he wants; the seven-year-old won't share his candy with others; the eight-year-old throws food at the table; the nine-year-old pushes other kids out of the way to be first in line for the cafeteria; the ten-year-old is supposed to say grace but instead makes a mockery of it by laughing and making up silly phrases; the eleven-year-old gives up on his math after two minutes because he thinks it's too hard.

This list could go on and on; and as you can see, these problems are not limited to the home. Like a virus, they show up in a variety ways and in a variety of settings and can negatively impact a child's life, both academically, with poor performance, and socially, with peer relationships.

Children with self-control problems often struggle in school. They may have a hard time paying attention in the classroom. They can feel so restless that sitting still is a challenge. They may be disruptive to the goings-on in the classroom. They may not finish their assignments, or they may hand in sloppy and careless work, or both. They may try to find the easy way out by copying the work of others. In short, their performance falls short because the normal requirements of life are too much for them.

These children typically relate poorly to their peers. They may want to be the center of attention and the first to participate in every activity. They may try to dominate and boss other kids around to get their way. They may be too aggressive, shoving and pushing and fighting. They may have a hard time sharing with others. As a result, they are often shunned by their peers. They may end up feeling like no one likes them, and their self-esteem suffers.

If young people enter adulthood with these problems, they will have difficulties in life because they will not have sufficient inner resources to be a responsible, mature person. Learning self-control, then, is critical to becoming a full-fledged adult.

Self-control is so critical to becoming a well-functioning adult that I have devoted this entire chapter to it. The first part focuses on what can happen in a family when children do not learn self-control, and then discusses ways for you to help your kids develop it.

ITS NEVER TOO EARLY AND ITS NOT TOO LATE

In my work with nursery schools and young families, I have learned how important it is to start teaching children self-control when they are young. Children, of course, are uncontrolled, and parents have to slowly and steadily teach them to contain themselves. The failure to do so can lead to unhappy results.

Ed and Carla consulted me about their middle child, thirteen-year-old Larry, who was refusing to attend school. He had also dropped out of soccer and baseball and, having hardly any friends, spent almost all of his time by himself. Ed and Carla were quite puzzled about his refusal to attend school. They didn't understand it. As we talked about the family, however, some interesting information emerged.

Their family was comprised of five children, with the two oldest living on their own. Larry was the oldest of the three at home. As we discussed the family situation, it became clear that there were discipline and mild behavior problems with all three of the children. For example, Larry and his younger sister and brother went to bed whenever they felt like it. There was not a regular, established bedtime, even for the youngest who was nine. Larry often went to bed after eleven on school nights.

Meals were helter-skelter, and Carla often cooked special meals for various members of the family on the same night. She felt like she was a "slave in the kitchen." The nine-year-old was argumentative and unwilling to follow directions. Moreover, the children had practically no chores and responsibilities around the home.

Their oldest child, who was now twenty, had begun to be rebellious when she was fourteen. She had stayed away from the family, at first for short periods, then for days at a time. There were times when Ed and Carla had no idea where she was. She finally "officially" left the family at sixteen to live on her own. Subsequently, she had been in relationships with abusive and alcoholic men, and presently was living in another town with her infant child.

What I found significant was that Ed and Carla told me that she had been defiant since she was three. Actually, they had never been able to manage her successfully, and she had been a behavior problem all through her childhood. When she reached adolescence, the problems reached a new level as she rebelled by staying away from home. Basically, she had become uncontrollable. One of the keys to understanding what had happened was that from the earliest age, she had not learned self-control.

You can see that these problems did not begin when their daughter reached fourteen. They just became more obvious. She had not had sufficient limits placed on her throughout her growing up. It is a clear example of how not dealing with day-to-day issues can lead to much more serious problems.

While there may have been other factors involved in these problems, the lack of limits and boundaries was a major reason for her rebelliousness. It is hard to overestimate the importance of training children early on to be responsible. It's never too early.

And it was not too late for Ed and Carla to help Larry and his brothers develop more self-control. They were clearly concerned that Larry was starting to act up at the same age as their older daughter, and they were frightened that they would have similar problems. They did not want to fall into the same traps again.

First, Ed and Carla made changes in their parenting styles. Carla tended to let things go and to accommodate the kids far too much. She was too permissive and her style was that of the pleasing parent. Ed would sit back, waiting until things got out of hand, and then would jump in with an authoritarian, heavy-handed approach. He would become angry and yell at the kids. "I'm the ogre," he said. He was frustrated and disheartened with his role in the family.

Neither Carla nor Ed used consequences to manage the kids. There simply weren't any. On the one hand, they placed very few demands on the kids, and on the other, they employed practically no consequences for misbehavior. You can readily see that the circumstances were not in place for these children to learn self-control.

Once they could see what was happening in the family more clearly, Ed and Carla made changes. First, the boys' mild oppositional styles were dealt with. They then assigned all the boys chores and established clear consequences. Routines for eating dinner, going to bed, and getting up were established. (Since the boys liked to stay up late, this became a privilege with which they were rewarded.) It took about two months before the household was running smoothly, and shortly after that Larry was back in school.

Ed and Carla had been having problems managing their children for many years, and when adolescence arrived, the problems jumped a few levels. The behavior problems and difficulty with self-control became much more difficult to handle. Unfortunately, this is not an unusual scenario. If Ed and Carla had known how to foster the development of self-control in the kids from early on, many problems would likely have been prevented. On the other hand, it was not too late to learn more effective tools to deal with the three children still at home, and this they did successfully.

FIVE WAYS TO HELP CHILDREN DEVELOP SELF-CONTROL

There are several ways to help children develop self-control. In one way or another, they all involve learning to deal with frustration. Kids need to learn to deal with the obstacles to getting what they want, without falling apart over it. Toddlers can't do this, but then we don't expect them to. But as children get older, they must be able to handle the frustrations that life puts in front of them. The ability to tolerate frustration is a gradually acquired trait. The passage of time helps, and we can help time do its job.

Back to the Basics—Responsibilities

Having responsibilities means that at times children have to put aside what they want to do. This is something adults must do on a regular basis, particularly parents; and children need to learn to do this little by little as they grow older. Having responsibilities is a basic building block of developing self-control.

By the middle of the second grade, Kendall was having a great deal of difficulty. He wasn't paying attention in class, frequently wandered around the classroom, and usually completed only part of his assignments and schoolwork. He didn't try very hard and was often observed throwing down his book or pencil in frustration. School testing had shown that Kendall was above average in intelligence, had no learning disabilities, and had no emotional problems.

However, his parents told me that he became frustrated very easily. In addition, it turned out that they so much wanted him to have a happy life that they gave in to him far too often. Moreover, he had few chores. Of course, there were times when he could not have his way and then would easily become upset.

Kendall was lacking in maturity, in the ability to take on increasingly more difficult tasks in life and to handle them appropriately. But this was not as bad as it sounds. All it took was the slow and steady introduction of chores and responsibilities at home and a change in parental style from a pleasing to a firm one in which there were clear limits, which in Kendall's case meant being told no at the appropriate times. Once the parents did this, Kendall learned to handle not getting what he wanted all the time and was able to tolerate frustration much better. Soon afterward, he began doing his schoolwork and completing his assignments.

When you stop and think about it, how can children handle more difficult challenges in life, such as being in school all day long and doing assignments and homework, if they are unable to do the little things in life, such as picking up their toys and making their beds? In order to do the things we consider important, the major tasks and challenges in life, we all have to be able to do the little things—the nitty-gritty, day-to-day tasks that are seemingly unimportant and often overlooked. It is essential for kids to do these tasks in order to build the skills needed for the big challenges in life.

The pleasing parental style is probably the one that contributes most to a child lacking self-control and being difficult to manage. I see it over and over again. The child in a family where this parenting style prevails does not get sufficient experience in the day-to-day requirements of life, and because of this lack of experience, does not develop the internal controls to handle the demands of life and the ordinary frustrations that life brings. These children easily become resentful and can develop oppositional styles. Therefore, be sure your children have age-appropriate rules and responsibilities (good old R and R) from an early age.

Responsibilities and Self-Control

Give your children age-appropriate, day-to-day responsibilities. This is a crucial way for them to build the inner resources needed to handle the frustrations and demands of life.

Back to Basics Again: Prevent Oppositional Styles from Forming

Having come this far in the book, you knew I wouldn't stray from this topic too long. There is nothing new here, except to tell you that eliminating negative and oppositional styles is a huge factor in enabling a child to develop self-control.

When a child regulates the way he or she talks to you, the child takes a giant step forward in being able to regulate all of her behavior. Controlling the style helps control emotions so that they do not get out of hand and cause problems. Why? The way a person relates emotionally runs through all of that person's reactions and, thus, affects all his behavior. An effective style helps generate the self-control needed in life.

Some people misunderstand what it means to control feelings. It does not mean getting rid of feelings. It is not about finding ways to push feelings away or to suppress them. When this happens, feelings just go underground, only to pop up again, sometimes at inopportune times. A child, indeed any person, must be able to handle emotions and express them effectively and constructively, so that emotions do not hinder her self-expression but rather serve it.

So once again, be sure that your child's style is appropriate and acceptable. This training will enable her to be an expressive and effective communicator. As a result, the child will be more in charge of herself and more able to relate well to others, with all the benefits that brings.

There is one caution: It is possible to go too far in this direction. You can overdo training in self-control. If you overdo training in self-control, your children may not feel free to express themselves and/or may become too inhibited. Encourage self-expression in a self-controlled way.

"Wait Training"

A characteristic that you can't miss noticing in children with self-control and behavior problems is that they can't wait. These kids can't wait for their turn, can't wait for recess, can't wait for dessert, can't wait when you are talking to someone else, can't wait to go out to play, and can't wait to get to where you are taking them. There is no end to the opportunities to wait in life. Having the capacity to wait is important.

Because kids with "wait" problems have to have what they want NOW, this moment is the only moment. These kids have never heard of the future. When they have to wait, they become easily upset. At the very least, they persistently pester and nag their parents: "When can we go to the park?" "When can I have ice cream?" The pestering then turns into demands: "I want to go to the park now." "I want some ice cream now."

Years ago, I lived on the edge of a forest, and woodpeckers would peck on the roof of my house, often at dawn. I would be sleeping peacefully, only to be awakened by what sounded like a jackhammer: RAT-A-TAT; RAT-A-TAT. On an emotional level, this is what it feels like when kids persistently nag and demand.

Once a parent has helped a child who is hard to manage become cooperative, there may still be some problems remaining with self-control, especially with waiting. One way to help children who can't wait is to introduce small waiting periods into their life. First, find out how long they can wait. What is their baseline tolerance for waiting? Start with something simple, such as dessert. Can a child wait thirty seconds, a minute, or five or ten minutes for dessert? The indicator will be the amount of upset, complaining, and pestering that occurs. If a child can't wait a minute without complaining or getting upset, then you know you have a problem on your hands.

Once you establish a baseline, simply increase it slightly and acknowledge your child for waiting. Take one issue at a time and slowly extend the waiting periods. If your child can only wait thirty seconds, try having her wait forty-five seconds. If successful, acknowledge her. The next time, increase it a little more.

Here is a summary of "Wait Training":

1. Establish a baseline through observation.
2. Increase the baseline in small steps.
3. Reward each step along the way.

At some point you can use "not waiting" as an additional reward: "I know you love the lemon meringue pie I made this morning, and I was going to serve it for dessert after dinner, but you have been doing such a good job of waiting lately that you don't have to wait for dinner. You can have some for dessert after lunch." Slowly, children can learn that waiting pays off.

Interrupting—A Special Case of "Not Waiting"

Many children fall into a habit of interrupting at some point in their young lives. (Being a keen observer, I've noticed that a few adults do this, too.) In fact, interrupting often starts soon after kids learn to talk and realize that they can get what they want by communicating. They think, "Hey, this works pretty good. I'm going to give this a run." So they just talk whenever they want, not realizing that they have to wait their turn.

They dart into a room and blurt out the latest event in their life, regardless of who is there and what is going on in the room. Or they march in on you when you're on the phone and blare their wants and needs. When you ignore them, they get louder. "Dad" becomes "DAD!" and so on. I don't have to say that a child's habitual interrupting tests our own ability to handle frustration.

This habit of interrupting is often part of a child's overall pattern of not waiting and not being able to handle frustration. Teaching a child not to interrupt will help him or her to wait and to handle frustration.

If you talk to your child when he interrupts, you are giving permission to the behavior and rewarding it, thereby training behavior that you don't want. As with many issues we have discussed in this book, the first thing is to be sure you do not reward the interrupting, although sometimes it just isn't possible. Just tell your child: "I am not going to respond to you when you interrupt." One of the main times children interrupt is when they want something. Put one of our old guidelines into play: They can't have something if you don't respond, and you won't respond when they interrupt.

Tell your kids: "Before you talk, look to see if I am already talking to someone first, or if I am busy, or if I am on the phone." Then acknowledge them for their attempts to do this. Learning to wait to speak is excellent training in the ability to tolerate frustration and, therefore, in the overall development of self-control.

Paying Attention to Others

Children with self-control problems tend to be concerned only with themselves. One way to help children develop self-control

Use the Stop-Sign Signal for Interruptions

This signal helps children break the interrupting habit. When they interrupt, simply put up your hand in the stop position and go on with your conversation. This can be used with any age but is particularly useful with younger children. Don't make a child wait too long, particularly at the beginning of this training. Just say, "Thanks for waiting. What do you want to tell me?"

---

consists in getting them out of themselves and focusing on others. They need to learn that they are not the sole inhabitants of earth, or at least that other people, as well as themselves, have needs and rights.

Here are three skills that you can help them to acquire:

1. *They need to listen to others.* Kids with self-control problems don't listen well to others because they are so preoccupied with what they want. Actually, they *are* listening, but only to themselves. Help your children listen to others.

   One simple way to do this is to ask them to repeat what you or someone else said: "What did I just say to you right now?" Or, "What did your brother ask you a minute ago?" See if they can tell you. If they can't, then encourage them to listen better and acknowledge them when they do. Use only positive consequences for this behavior, and don't introduce any logical consequences.

2. *They need to pay attention to their impact on others.* Kids who are self-centered don't pay attention to how they affect other people, and some training in this regard can be helpful to them.

   You can take any problem and ask them to reflect on it. Suppose you walk into your living room to find a dirty bicycle parked next to the couch. In addition to the techniques we have discussed in previous chapters, it would be useful to ask them to look at the impact of what they have done. You can ask them to examine the dirty rug that has tire marks and dirt on it and see if they understand what would be involved in cleaning it up. Then let them clean it up, or at least help.

Equally important is that you ask them to tell you how they think you *felt* when you discovered the bike and the dirty rug. If they can't tell you, then tell them the problems that the dirty bike causes for you and how it makes you feel. Avoid being judgmental and assure them that you know they didn't mean it, but it upset you anyway.

You can do this with peers also: "How do you think Tammy felt when you called her a moron?" "How do you think Andy felt when you borrowed his bat without asking him?"

This is training in empathy, the ability to put oneself in another's place and experience the world through his or her eyes. Do this gently and without any pressure, realizing that it takes some time to learn this trait.

3. *They need to acquire manners.* This is still another way to help children learn to pay attention to and to treat others respectfully. I won't go into details of how to do this, because I know you know how. I just want to emphasize its importance in this context. When children have good manners, they pay attention to others. They are more respectful and courteous and are more likely to treat others fairly—and they are able to control themselves.

Attaining self-control is critical in becoming a mature person. Being mature leads to being masterful in life. Do all you can to encourage the development of this trait in your kids. Although they may never thank you for it, the thanks will be there when you see them succeed as human beings.

CHAPTER SEVENTEEN

How Effective Discipline Helps Children Develop Self-Esteem and "Response-ability"

*I*magine for a moment that you have finished raising your children. A large portion of your life, twenty years or more, has been spent in this endeavor. Seeing your children become happy, competent adults gives you a wonderful feeling of satisfaction. Few experiences in life are so rewarding.

This book has addressed only one aspect of parenting, albeit a crucial one, the art of discipline. We easily overlook how powerful this process is. Over the course of the childrearing years, parents must discipline their children thousands and thousands of times. Probably because it occurs so often, discipline has an enormous impact on family life.

It is hoped that you are now using what you have learned to manage your children and to correct any problems that previously existed. You have made your share of mistakes, and being only human, will make some more; but you know it is not necessary to be perfect. There is plenty of room for error, and it is seldom too late to correct mistakes. When you manage your children effectively, your home will run more smoothly, there will be fewer conflicts, and everyone will be happier.

Moreover, when you manage your children effectively, your children will benefit in some ways that you may not have known about, much less anticipated. Effective discipline plays an important role in helping children to develop higher self-esteem and to develop a sense of competency in themselves. These traits enable kids to become successful, happy adults.

SELF-ESTEEM

Managing your children effectively helps them develop good self-esteem. If the notion of self-esteem seems a bit mysterious to you, that's understandable, because it is not something you can see directly. It is a quality that we infer from a person's behavior and actions. Self-esteem is basically what people think of themselves, how well, or poorly, as the case may be, they regard themselves. If a person thinks he is a likeable, capable person, then he will value himself, and his self-esteem will be high. On the other hand, to whatever degree he thinks that he is not likeable or capable, his self-esteem will be correspondingly lower. To complicate this a bit further, this estimation of the self is not necessarily on a conscious level. A person may not be aware of how she sees herself.

Researchers have discovered some interesting things about self-esteem. For one thing, it is linked to patterns of childrearing. In a study of boys, ages ten through twelve, it was found that their high self-esteem was related to a pattern of parenting similar to the firm, gentle style. Their parents displayed three characteristics in raising their sons:

1. Acceptance
2. Clearly defined limits
3. Respect for individuality

The first two of these characteristics are directly related to the two basic parenting skills needed to discipline and manage children effectively that we have been discussing in this book. These skills—effective relating and clear limit setting—help to foster self-esteem in children by building inner resources that are vital in order to get along in this world. When parents relate effectively to their children and set clear limits, children are able to accept themselves and develop a sense of competency.

EFFECTIVE RELATING AND SELF-ACCEPTANCE IN CHILDREN

When parents use the firm, gentle style to discipline their children, children feel accepted and supported, even when they have misbehaved. This parenting style gives them the message that they are okay. The kids come to understand that although in a given situation their behavior may not be acceptable, they are. This is not a "logical knowing." It is an emotional response. It is something they feel, and, therefore, it is something that tends to run deeply within.

The most important factor in determining how a child will feel during discipline is your parenting style. It is your style that impacts others, and in the discipline situation, it is your style that impacts your children. The firm, gentle style enables children to feel accepted and loved, which in turn enhances their self-esteem.

Some parenting styles can have negative emotional effects on children and on their self-esteem. A critical style, for example, can make a child think: "I can't do anything right." "I'm a failure." "I'm not good enough." "I'm not acceptable." As time goes by, these statements become conclusions about the self, about the child's identity.

Unfortunately, over the course of a childhood, these conclusions can become so strong that it is as though they are set in concrete, and they become hard to get rid of. They become part of how the child defines herself, and her self-esteem suffers accordingly. Even though a parent does not intend this outcome, a critical style can make a child feel this way. Remember that in relating, it is the *style* that impacts others and produces the emotional result, not the intention.

Another style that negatively impacts self-esteem is the victim or martyr style, which can make children feel guilty. In this case, children conclude that "I am bad," and this statement becomes part of the way they see themselves, with a corresponding loss of self-esteem. Over the years, I have worked with innumerable adults suffering from excessive guilt and a pervasive inner sense that they are bad, when in actuality they are far from it. We have often traced this guilt back to the victim/martyr style of their parents.

You can see, then, how important your style is, not just in managing your children but in the impact it has on their emotional well-being. When you employ a firm, gentle style that supports and accepts your children, it helps them feel good about themselves and their sense of who they are, which will remain intact even when you must correct their behavior and give them consequences.

On the other side of the relating pattern is the way your child talks to you. Another reason, besides that of maintaining discipline, that you do not want a child's negative way of talking and relating to develop into an oppositional style is that the child is acquiring poor interpersonal skills that make it difficult to have good relationships with others. This interferes with a sense of relatedness to others and affects self-esteem. People simply cannot feel good about themselves when they do not have good relationships. Moreover, when parents relate effectively, they model good interpersonal skills for their children.

When parents and their children relate well, they feel close to each other and enjoy each other. The children are then likely to identify with their parents. They accept their values and internalize their standards and requirements more readily, making them want to cooperate so that managing them goes even more smoothly.

SETTING LIMITS AND
A SENSE OF COMPETENCY

Clear, firm limits and consequences enable children to feel secure because they know where the boundaries are and what is expected of them. In the study mentioned earlier, the researchers also found that enforcement of limits gives a child a sense that norms are real and important, and this contributes to a child's self-definition.

Moreover, when these boundaries are neither too confining nor too broad, children have a certain kind of freedom. They can explore their world and try new things, knowing that they are secure. This makes it easier for them to develop resources and ultimately have successes. They find that they are capable people.

Through this safe exploration, they develop inner "I can" statements about themselves:

"I can solve problems."
"I can make decisions."
"I can persist."
"I can learn."
"I can take risks."
"I can _____."

"I can" is an inner statement of mastery; and while kids may not make these statements in the adult language described here, they do develop a larger sense that they are capable and can deal with life. Competency is not just about having successes in the world; it is also about having a sense of being in charge of one's life and having the resources within oneself to cope.

A common misunderstanding about self-esteem is that it consists in performance and achievement, and we live in a society that highly rewards accomplishments. There is nothing inherently wrong with this, except that many children are taught both directly and indirectly from a very early age that the more they do and the better they perform, the more worth-while they are. Therefore, the higher their grades and the bet-ter their athletic performance, the more acceptable and loveable they are as people. In adults, this can manifest as the more money one has and the higher one rises in the corpora-tion, or whatever way one performs to feel good about the self, the more worthwhile that person is.

While not everyone operates under this imperative, many peo-ple in our society do, and it can set up a situation in which they become driven to perform. When people are driven, however, they can never do enough to satisfy themselves. I remember an acquaintance of mine many years ago who was a director in a large corporation and who was making a great deal of money, and yet was not satisfied with himself. A few years later, I ran into him. He had established a consulting business and was making even more money than when I had last seen him, and he still expressed dissatisfaction with his life and, by implication, himself.

When people are driven to perform and to achieve in order to feel good about themselves, the sad fact is that they can never feel good about themselves. They are trapped in a need to accomplish, and there is always more to accomplish. They see that they are not accomplishing those other things, and they feel dissatisfied with themselves.

Self-esteem is not about performance in and of itself. If it is dependent on what is outside the self, it can never be enough. Self-esteem is an internal matter. It is a sense in the self that one is acceptable and worthwhile no matter what happens. People doing even the lowest paying jobs can have high self-esteem. They can like themselves and believe they are capable because they have that inner sense of mastery.

When you set boundaries effectively, an additional benefit for your children is that they can explore their world safely and in the process learn about themselves and who they are. The almost magical aspect is that they can even say to themselves, "I can fail; I can make mistakes and it is all right." When they do this, they are developing a sense of competency in themselves, a sense that is unrelated to how any particular endeavor turns out. The paradox is that because they can fail and still feel good about themselves, they are much more likely to be competent and succeed.

RESPONSIBILITY AND "RESPONSE-ABILITY"

Another way of looking at the above discussion is that children who have a sense of "I can" develop the ability to respond to a wide variety of situations and challenges. They are "response-able" because through having the freedom to explore within well-defined boundaries that are neither too small nor too large, they develop a sense in themselves that they possess the inner resources to cope in life.

Responsibility is a key ingredient of the mature individual. A central part of responsibility is the ability to delay gratification. You do it all the time. You take care of the demands of life and your household, you put off your own needs, and sometimes it is ten o'clock at night before you can really sit down for a moment to rest and relax. (Is it midnight? Sorry.)

A few years ago researchers studied what happened to those children who were able to delay gratification and those who were not. Using marshmallows, they brought four-year-olds into a room and told them that they could have the marshmallow right then, but if they waited until the researcher came back, they could have two of them.

Some children ate the marshmallow as soon as the researcher closed the door. Others squirmed and went through contortions as they tried not to eat the marshmallow. It apparently was amusing to watch (the researchers were watching through a one-way mirror) but undoubtedly not so amusing for those poor kids. However, it was worth it, because when he came back, the researcher gave the children who held out their extra marshmallow.

When the children in the study reached high school, the researchers surveyed their parents and teachers. What they discovered was that the children who could wait, who could delay gratifying themselves for a bigger reward, were better adjusted, more dependable, and more confident. The children who could not wait were more likely to be easily frustrated, to be stubborn, and to be lonely. Moreover, the kids who waited scored much higher on the Scholastic Aptitude Test by an average of 210 points. That is a huge difference.

When you discipline your children, you are automatically teaching them to be responsible; and at the same time, they are learning to delay gratification, a trait that apparently has a lot to do with success. Over time, your child internalizes this trait and gains a larger perspective, one that serves her well in life. This is one example, then, of the effects of discipline beyond simply having the household run smoothly. The ability of children to delay gratification, in addition to being a central characteristic of a mature person, has profound long-term effects on success in life.

This study suggests that responsible children, those who are able to delay gratification, also have response-ability. This is an inner sense of capability, a sense of mastery in life, the ability to face and meet the circumstances and challenges that life gives us. In a very real way, responsibility helps children become more response-able.

Chronically uncooperative and hard-to-manage children are neither happy nor successful precisely because they are not responsible. They have all kinds of difficulties in self-control and in relating to others, and usually have poor self-esteem as well. These children are often described as lacking in maturity, and they typically do not meet their obligations either at home or at school. In addition, they have a much harder time learning to be adaptable and to develop the resources they need to cope and to manage their lives.

On the other hand, when children are cooperative and responsible, their lives are more likely to go well. Compared with uncooperative kids, they are more independent, resourceful, resilient, initiating, persevering, and forward-looking. Because they are more sensitive to and considerate of others, they relate to others more effectively. As the research showed, they are happier and better adjusted than uncooperative children.

Because they internalize these behaviors and their parents' values, as responsible children grow, they handle life's challenges maturely. They are able to choose like-minded friends, for example, and are much more likely to avoid temptations, such as using drugs.

Responsibility also means that children are accountable for how they relate to others. In hard-to-manage children, resistive and oppositional styles not only are manipulative and interfere with cooperative behavior but also create problems in relating. Children cannot have good interpersonal relationships with others when they relate in an oppositional manner.

Thus, when parents are effective in setting limits and in the process relate effectively to their kids, their children benefit tremendously. Because maturation proceeds more smoothly, children become more response-able and resourceful and are more likely to be happy and successful.

Moreover, your job becomes much easier in the long run and you enjoy your children. When you manage your children successfully, you have an inner feeling of satisfaction. Your own self-esteem will be higher when you have mature, responsible, and response-able kids.

MORE WAYS TO DEVELOP RESPONSIBILITY AND "RESPONSE-ABILITY"

Additional ways to develop a sense of responsibility in children include promoting choices and involving them in selected family decisions.

Promoting Choices

It's a hot summer day and seven-year-old Alex is bored. "I don't have anything to do," he tells Mom. In this situation, the first choice belongs to Mom. She can tell Alex what to do, or she can help him create ideas about what he might do and then let him make the choice. She chose to help Alex make his own choices.

She sat down with her son, and they brainstormed what Alex could do that day. "Why don't you get a pencil and a piece of paper, and we'll write down the ideas that we come up with," Mom suggested. Together, they came up with a list of eleven things that Alex could do that day.

"Now, what do you want to do?" asked Mom.
"I don't know," replied Alex.
"You're the only one who can decide," rejoined his wise mom.

She was wise because she knew that Alex's boredom was his problem, not hers. She had helped him get to the point where he had some ideas. The next move was his. He could try one or more of the possibilities, or not; but it was up to him, not her. She knew it was Alex's responsibility to create a "non-bored" day for himself. She was there for him and encouraging, but the responsibility was his.

By giving him *responsibility* for his boredom and for creating his day, Alex's mother was also helping him to find *response-able* solutions to his life situation, in this particular case his having nothing to do. Rather than being dependent on Mom to figure it out for him, Alex now had the opportunity to try out a number of possibilities to make his day go well. By trying these possibilities in this tiny slice of life, he would be relying on himself and would be learning to be persevering and resilient. When this type of response happens hundreds of times in a child's life, it has an important effect, because it establishes a pattern.

Another suggestion, one that was discussed previously but bears repeating, is to give kids choices when it comes to doing chores and handling consequences for their behavior.

When you give your children choices and help them develop their own, they can gradually learn to make the connection between what they decide and what happens. In the situation with Alex, once he could see what possibilities he had he could see that how his day went was up to him and only up to him.

Contributing to the Family

Chores are an important part of family life. A family is a miniature community in which everyone gives and receives. Even very young children, roughly from age three on, should contribute to the running of the family. For the three-year-old, it may mean picking up her toys with Dad's help; and for the twelve-year-old it may mean major responsibilities in the cleaning-of-the-house department.

When children have chores to do, they are contributing significantly to family life, and it is important to let them know that they have a contribution to make. Let them know the effects that their contributions have, and let them know how much it helps you. They then have a sense of inclusiveness, of belonging and being a part of something larger than themselves. This will enhance their self-esteem.

Input is also important; it is another way that children can contribute to the family. Involve them in selected family decisions and ask them for their ideas and solutions. Occasionally, you can give them some responsibility for coming up with solutions.

Suppose that the family decides to take up camping, but no one knows much about it. You can take one or more of the kids to the library and find age-appropriate books on camping for the kids to read. For example, they can contribute by coming up with ideas about the kind of tent to buy and the places to go. They take on a small piece of the responsibility for creating a camping vacation and in so doing feel not only a strong sense of involvement in the family but also a sense of resourcefulness in themselves, that they can find solutions and meet challenges. They are responsible and response-able.

RESPECT FOR INDIVIDUALITY

This is the third quality that the researchers found in childrearing practices that contributes to good self-esteem. Although it is not part of the disciplinary process as such, it is worth mentioning because it is so important. You can enhance your children's self-esteem by encouraging and promoting their individuality. You can help them see what it is in themselves that makes them unique and help them to develop those qualities and traits.

One powerful way to do this is to encourage their self-expression. Let them say what they think and let them know you respect them, even when you don't agree with their views and ideas. Encourage them to think for themselves, to be creative and to try new things.

You now have a variety of tools for disciplining your children effectively and for maintaining satisfying relationships with them. Relating and discipline are everyday events, and it is important to stay aware and attend to them everyday. It is human nature to slip back into old ways of doing things, because we think it is easier. Believe me, in the long run it is not. Stay on top of the patterns, and you and your kids will be much happier.

Finally, I urge you to make your kids your number one priority. In today's crazily busy world, this is not easy to do. Everyone I talk to complains about how much they have to do. I fear that as a society we are losing track of our priorities. It is easy to move children down the list.

Spend time with your children. Share yourself with them. They need to know that *they* are your priority. They will feel special and loved.

For information on scheduling workshops and talks by Dr. Garvey, please call: (408) 379-8270

INDEX